Habiba Jessica Zaman-Tran has a Master's degree in Professional Counseling specializing in trauma. She is the therapist and owner of North Star of Georgia Counseling. With 15 years of experience working in the counseling field, including counseling, advocacy, guidance and education, she believes that as a person becomes more aware of their fears, perception, desires and strengths, they can make successful life changes. She is author of 10 publications including a children's book published in 2012 titled *But I'm Just Playing*. Habiba is of Bangladeshi and American descent. She has two children and lives in Atlanta, Georgia with her family.

Shalon M. Irving, PhD, MPH, MS, CHES, Lieutenant Commander in the United States Public Health Service, focused her work on the development and implementation of community-based participatory approaches to community health improvement, with specific emphasis on improving health outcomes for urban African– American women from their adolescence to middle-adulthood. She was an educator, scientist, author, devoted friend, loyal daughter and loving mother. *Shalon Irving passed away January 27th, 2017.*

Dedication

To Shalon Irving. She was tenacious and unrelenting in this endeavor because she believed in this message and she believed in me. She was determined to bring to others the understanding, peace, and self-love she worked so hard to achieve. I could not have done this without her.

Habiba Zaman-Tran and Shalon
Irving

BEAUTIFULLY BARE
UNDENIABLY YOU

AUSTIN MACAULEY PUBLISHERS™

London * Cambridge * New York * Sharjah

Ordering Information:
Quantity sales: special discounts are available on quantity purchases by corporations, associations, and others. For details, contact the publisher at the address below.

Publisher's Cataloguing-in-Publication data
Zaman-Tran Habiba and Irving Shalon.
Beautifully Bare Undeniably You

ISBN 9781641820790 (Paperback)
ISBN 9781641820783 (Hardback)
ISBN 9781641820776 (E-Book)

The main category of the book — Biography & Autobiography/General

www.austinmacauley.com

First Published (2018)
Austin Macauley Publishers Ltd™
40 Wall Street, 28th Floor
New York, NY 10005
USA
mail-usa@austinmacauley.com
+1 (646) 5125767

Table of Content

Jill Scott

*For the first time I've allowed someone, no you, to
strip me of all my clothing, all my confusion, all my doubts, all
my fear of love
and life.
I am Naked. Yes naked. Butt naked and
impressed with your ability to see me,
to see ME
clearly
through my private lonely haze.
You touch me.
You feel me and make me tremble with the
possibilities of
Tomorrow, the next day and the next day.
With you
I feel my cloud cleared
my rain washing me.
With you
my flower blooms in December cold
with you
I lose mental chaos and gain tranquility.
You have my power and when I grow weary,
you replenish me.
With you
my angry ocean sits placid calm
with you
I have become
my entire self.*

No matter how far down the path you go, you can always turn around…

1. Introduction
The Process of Change

Many people are generally satisfied with the material and social circumstances of their lives. They have sufficient money, good health, steady jobs, good friends, and successful relationships. But that does not mean that all of their aspirations in life have been fulfilled. When they realize that, even with their general sense of life satisfaction something is still missing, they look for ways to expand their personalities, to grow psychologically or even spiritually, seeking to change in some way with the goal of becoming a better, happier person.

Change means reinvention or reincarnation, an opportunity to become different or start anew. Change is not inevitable—it is an opportunity *and* it is a choice. Each time a shift happens in our lives, whether major or minor, we have to take control of who we will become or we risk never reaching our full potential. This process is not automatic, rather, we have to choose the path of reincarnation—deliberately and with foresight. The alternative to actively choosing change is stagnation, which many of us have experienced on one or more occasions. For myself, when I've waited for my future to find me, I've waited in vain, lost in confusion and sadness.

Sometimes we know, without a shadow of a doubt, that some aspect of our life needs to change. In those instances, we may even know how to change it and be able to easily embark on the journey towards change. There are other times when the movement towards change is not so clear and well-articulated. But rest assured, there are many ways to tell if it is time for a change, including:

- When the way you feel is affecting your sleep, appetite, job or relationships.
- When, despite your best efforts, things are not getting better.
- When you can't find the answers to your problems.
- You feel an overwhelming and prolonged sense of sadness, helplessness, or hopelessness.
- When emotional difficulties make it hard for you to function and engage fully from day to day.
- You recognize (or someone points out) that your actions are harmful to yourself or others around you.
- You are troubled by problems facing family members or close friends.
- You find it difficult or impossible to prioritize what is most important in your life.

We may experience one or more of these triggers for change; sometimes the triggers are fleeting and other times they stick around and become constant, nagging reminders that something in your life is not as it should be. We can, and frequently do, ignore the triggers for a long time, choosing to focus on something else, continuing to try the same strategies to deal with our issues, or temporarily giving up and resigning ourselves to our current situation. However, it is at the moment when we can no longer ignore the triggers, and the realization that we need a change becomes apparent and won't go away, that we choose to do something different, to start the process or journey towards a better, fuller, and happier existence.

"Looking back, I realize that I could not start the process of change until I stopped viewing myself as irreparable. It turns out that realizing that the way I viewed myself was flawed and holding me back, was my catalyst for change. I don't know exactly when or how I adopted this point of view. No one ever explicitly told me I was broken—for an ex, once in the heat of an argument—but I never needed the words to be spoken to get the message. I often felt like my heart and spirit had been shattered into a thousand different pieces and most days I was just barely

holding myself together with duct tape, Krazy glue, and sheer fear of falling totally apart. Oddly enough, it was that fear, in part, that motivated me to get better.

For years, I was scared shitless of hitting rock bottom. The fear of having things fall totally apart led me to realize that there must still be something left to break. Yes, I had experienced my share of trauma, but there were pieces of me that I still held sacred and considered were worthy of protecting—and recognizing that was huge! I've only recently gotten to a point of honestly being able to say I am perfect. I say this, not a statement of conceit or even one born from having drawn comparisons to others, because trust me, I am flawed beyond belief. I still almost daily make mistakes and questionable choices. I am a procrastinator and am rather messy. I love French fries. My thighs could be smaller and my bank account larger. Yet, I feel thankful and blessed.

This is the life that I have carefully crafted and exists solely based on my truths. I have stopped believing the lies fed to me by the outside world, social media, friends, and other people's expectations, and have begun to reject alternative truths that do not coincide with my own. I no longer entertain conversations about why this person thinks my lifestyle is wrong or why that one thinks I should grow my hair longer...eat more meat...live in that neighborhood. Or just be different. I am who I am and she is perfect."

Reinvention starts at the mind. It will be neither easy nor seamless and there will be times when you want to quit, simply because it is too hard and you feel exhausted. From the very beginning of the process, you must recognize that it will not be possible to reinvent yourself if you remain stuck in the same old thinking patterns. It will be necessary to actively rally against the negative thinking that may have kept you stuck for so long. We realize that this may sound daunting and, honestly, it may even feel impossible at times. But, what you will quickly find as you move forward on the journey towards your ideal self, is that once you make it a practice, it will become easier to identify ways to improve some of the aspects of your thinking, in both large and small ways. There will, of course, be setbacks and you may even be tempted to go back to your old patterns, no matter how unhealthy or damaging they may have been. So don't be alarmed. And don't beat yourself up if you slip. Just remember that this is all a choice and the next time those same feelings arise, choose differently.

There are times when we encounter resistance, unfortunately it does not come only from the outside world; frequently, our most powerful adversary to change is found within. We don't want to let go, even of things that cause us pain or that are obviously already out of our grasp. In fact, there may be times when you find yourself actively holding on to the pain just because it is familiar and may even feel comfortable, like an old sweater.

As we were writing this book, we encountered a saying about walking away and learning to stop watering dead flowers expecting them to grow. Yet we, like others, have spent countless hours in front of metaphorical gardens tending to dead and decaying flowers and plants as if the sheer power of our love or dedication would bring them back to life, when in reality, the best solution would be to pull the dead things up from their root, discard them, and move on so that we have a chance to plant and harvest something new. We may also struggle with limiting beliefs and messages about ourselves that hold us back from trying new things. Those timeless narratives that tell you that 'you aren't good enough so why even try' may play over and over in your head as if on repeat when you are in the process of change. Much like the flowers, it is necessary to stop the 'tape', throw it out, and walk away towards something greater—to the you that you are meant to be and not who you have been told that you are.

Before you can reinvent yourself, you have to know who you currently are (and maybe have some idea about who you would like to be). We must find a connection between what really matters to us and the goals we chase. Of course growth will mean different things to everyone. For some, it means greater freedom to do what they want, live as they want, and pursue their interests. Others seek to understand themselves better, develop their personal capacities, and experience new things. Some want to search within themselves for some deeper truer self or psyche. It would seem, however, that growth in whatever way you define it shares a single underlying theme: the common thread of expanding yourself and your world to make it more of what you want and less of what you don't (yes, even that is within your control).

Those reading this book are in search of some type of change in their lives. While each of us is seeking a change or reincarnation unique to us and our experiences and desires, there are some universal characteristics. For example, components such as pain and healing or struggle and growth that help you move from where you currently are to where you want to be are common themes present in the process of change. As awareness of one's fears, perception, desires and strengths increase, successful life change becomes infinitely more possible.

Like us, you may have grown tired of traditional self-help books, articles, and blogs with their self-proclaimed experts. Although we already had the idea to write the book, our impetus to begin putting pen to paper was after reading, and subsequently laughing at, a seriously misinformed attempt to empower women to be happier through submission. As we started to examine this and other sources of self-help information, we realized that what they had in common was generic suggestions, little detailed guidance to help you through the process, and a professional distance that while objective, did not feel overly helpful. Hence, our motivation to begin was not from our soapbox shrouded expertise and professionalism, although between us we have significant training and expertise in psychology, sociology, and health education across the life course. Instead, we decided to talk to you as we talk to one another. Grounded in our personal experiences and honesty, we want to empower and support your change process because we believe that you are powerful and have the capacity to manifest the 'you' of your dreams.

This book will first and foremost be a place for us to share our many attempts at getting it right…and some of the instances where we've gotten it horribly wrong. We are willing to lay bare our lives with all of our questionable choices and painful growth.

We will even delve into those stagnant times that could conceivably stretch from days to weeks to months to whole careers. In that sense, it is as much therapeutic for us as we hope it will be transformative for you, the reader. Throughout our stories, we will show you the strategies and skills that we have mastered to get out of our ruts and live the best versions of ourselves.

Self-awareness, or the process of becoming more honest with ourselves, can initiate the authenticity that often results in healing, transformation and your ability to lead a fuller life. Throughout this book, our goal is to provide guidance, examples, and activities to help you actualize the growth you desire. We will walk with you throughout this journey of identifying issues, establishing goals, and becoming increasingly aware of recurring patterns that may be hindering your growth.

Psychotherapy is just that—a step-by-step process to help guide those in need of a change. First, and most importantly, psychotherapy is a relationship. Second, it is a relationship with a purpose. And finally, it is a purposeful relationship that is willingly established. Although we will not be physically working together, our goal is to accompany you through a journey of self-discovery and reliance as if you were walking with us through this process. You will get to know each of us, our history of pain, longing, growth, disappointment, fear, and healing. You will read our stories and understand our paths to healing, including our stumbling blocks along the way. Ultimately, you will gain an in-depth understanding of different applications that can be used to reach that potential.

"I cannot remember the last time I felt like someone really saw me. If I'm honest, I don't know if that has ever truly happened. I imagine that when it happens it will be magical. Scary, but awesome in the sense that someone will finally 'get me'. I have been waiting so long for someone to be able to see through all of my pain and bravado. I was told once that no one would ever be able to do that until I was ready to present myself unashamed and unapologetic to the world. This resonated with me because for so long I had cultivated a practice of doing just

the opposite. I am an expert at hiding myself, at fitting into crowds and projecting a brusque and carefree persona so that no one could ever fathom my secrets.

I had gotten so good at it that there were times that I had hidden my true essence not only from the world but from myself, as well. Those times in my life have been the hardest—countless moments spent staring at my reflection in the mirror searching for some sense of recognition, some notion that the person staring back at me was real and represented the little girl I had been and the woman I was becoming. There have been days when I've stared for hours and felt nothing. No sense of recognition. No connection. Nothing. Those moments have been impossible. They're much rarer now and I hope that means that I am reconnecting with who I am and learning to face the pains and disappointments of life head-on instead of hiding and repressing them. It is that same sense of relief at being able to begin recognizing myself in the mirror that has sparked the desire to be seen by another, but my fear of exposing myself is so great.

Opening yourself up in the manner necessary to be seen involves risk, vulnerability and more than a little trust. I have always thought the hardest of these for me was vulnerability. I have always taken pride in the fact that people think of me as tough. I was raised with brothers and learned early on that crying is a sign of weakness and life has shown me over and over that people exploit perceived weaknesses for their own gain. For many years, I loathed feeling vulnerable. It was only recently that I realized that vulnerability is not the polar opposite of being strong. That is not why I feared it and avoided it. My fear and avoidance were motivated by the fact that fundamentally I don't trust people. I feel that in opening myself up, there will be judgment and possibly some form of punishment for showing my true self. I am not confident that I can display my vulnerability to the world without it being exploited. Yet, my desire to be 'seen' persists.

These two things—my fear and my desire—seem like such harsh contradictions and at their most basic level they may be. However, what I have determined is that there are parts of me that are not for public consumption. The trust that is required for *me to be able to open up and allow those parts of me to be visible is not freely given, it is earned, and must precede any efforts on my part to be transparent. For the person who earns the right to be trusted, I will, hopefully, be able to show myself. Maybe not all at once, but eventually, I will be able to step out of the shadows, put down the personas, and start dismantling the walls and moats and barricades placed strategically around my heart and emotions and fears. To the world I may still be cloaked in mystery—and I am okay with that. But to the chosen person or persons, I will be bare and unashamed."*

While we have not strayed away from using technical language to ground this process of change and discovery, we have made every attempt to avoid that 'textbook' jargon heavy feeling, choosing instead to make the book as readable and relatable as possible. So, bear with us when we get technical; we aren't trying to diagnose or scare you away. As you will quickly find, we transition easily between our personal and professional voices.

How You Learn to Live Alone, Bowen & Palladio

First you fall then you fly
And you believe that you belong up in the sky
Flap your arms as you run, every revolution
Brings you closer to the sun
You fall asleep in motion in uncharted hemispheres
And wake up with the stars falling down around your ears
When they hit the ground, they're nothing but stones
That's how you learn to live alone

Bit by bit, you slip away
You lose yourself in pieces in the things that you don't say
You're not here, but you're still there
The sun goes up, the sun goes down
And you're not sure you care
You live inside the false, till you don't recognize the true
People send you pictures, and you can't believe it's you
It's been years since your house has felt like home
That's how you learn to live alone

It don't feel right, but it's not wrong
It's just hard to start again this far along
Brick by brick, the letting go
As you walk away from everything you know
You release resistance, lean into the wind
Till the roof begins to crumble and the rain comes pouring
in

And you sit there in the rubble, till the rubble feels like
home
That's how you learn to live alone...

2. Forming
Let's Get This Party Started

As we stated in the first section, change is a choice. As you likely know from personal experience or have witnessed in the world around you, individuals can remain stuck in cycles of dependency, sadness, and destruction for lifetimes if they don't choose to do something to change. As much as we may find ourselves unhappy with our life, we have to choose to make it different. Once the choice is made and we are ready to move forward, we finally arrive at a place where we can begin. The first step is commitment.

Commitment

In this early phase, you may experience a range of emotions. It is common to feel extremely motivated on your process or journey towards change, but it is equally possible that you will feel anxious and a bit nervous—as it is difficult to fully grasp and understand the work we are about to embark on. The sole focus of this phase is to become familiar with yourself and your purpose. If, like so many of us, you have spent long spans of time trying to silence or ignore your own inner truths, choosing instead to live the life that someone else has wanted or envisioned for you, then this may feel a little uncomfortable.

It is important to acknowledge and accept that all of these feelings and emotions are completely normal. When you encounter feelings that may fuel the familiar urge to run, hide, or change direction, remember, if this were an easy process, it would be something innate that we, as humans, would engage in primarily without much thought or effort. It is unlikely to be easy but will be worthwhile. Once you commit, you will learn about opportunities and challenges and then agree on goals to work towards.

In the phase, we make several commitments to you as well. While we cannot process for you or provide the motivation that must come from within, we can provide guidance and companionship along the way and share insights from our lives to demonstrate our process. We will be transparent and honest in hopes that in seeing our reincarnations and reinventions, you will continue to strengthen your resolve to arrive at your own.

We will, with our (sometimes) eloquent prose, take you right to the edge of our personal shitholes and provide examples of how we have emerged. We are not disillusioned. We recognize that this type of resurrection happens under one of two very unique circumstances. Either someone you love pulls you— typically kicking and screaming—to the point of change, because your shit is now affecting them or they have grown genuinely concerned about your pain, suffering or general well-being. Or, the more sustainable alternative, you have reached a point where you are so discontent with the stagnation or trauma you are experiencing in one or more dimensions of your life, that you have mustered the courage and resolve to pull yourself out of the past into a bold new future. Regardless of the path that has brought you here—to this book, this page, and to this portion of your journey—we welcome you.

***

Awareness

Let's begin by taking a close look at some of the symptoms you may have been experiencing that reflect your suffering. When we use the word 'symptoms', it is not in the same clinical sense that you may be familiar with when discussing mental and emotional well-being. Instead, we are using the term to reflect recent physical or emotional struggles.

This list is simply meant to be a launch pad, or a way for us to begin focusing in on how you have been feeling. It is not meant to be comprehensive; for many of us, this list only begins to scratch the surface of the range of emotions we may have experienced or are currently experiencing. First, examine the symptoms listed below and identify those that have been concerning to you within the last year or so.

Nervousness	Memory	Alcohol/Drug Use
Friends	Finances	Children
Self-Control	Career Choices	Temper
Sexual Problems	Changes In Energy	Separation
Stomach Trouble	Unusual Sounds	Being a Parent
Relaxation	Health Problems	Nightmares
Concentration	Restricting	Stress
Decision Making	Unusual Visuals	Legal Matters
Education	Loneliness	Insomnia
Purging/ Binging	Feelings of Inferiority	My thoughts
Depression	Headaches	Divorce
Suicidal Ideation	Unhappiness	Marriage
Ambition	Work	Fears

It is expected that some of these symptoms will resonate with you more than others. Some you may have been aware of and others you may just be acknowledging for the first time. While these may or may not come as a surprise to you, sometimes, just seeing our 'symptoms' presented in black and white, can elicit an emotional response. Although we often try to suppress those emotions for fear of 'losing it' or showing weakness, we ask you to fight that instinct. Instead, allow yourself to fully experience any emotions that may wash over you, recognizing that (1) it is okay to feel and (2) by doing so you will lose nothing.

Whether you identified one symptom or many, the purpose of this activity was not to highlight what is wrong; rather, the activity helps to create connections and awareness—a process that occurs when we begin to associate specific experiences with the emotions that cause us suffering. While we are sometimes hesitant to embrace these emotional connections, they are necessary because we cannot change that of which we are not aware. And, it is only when we truly become aware of what we want, don't want and are unwilling to accept, that we arrive at a place where we can improve and grow. When we become aware, we begin to occupy a space where we have the ability to become better...although still imperfect.

There are two truths that are important to remember as we move towards our goals of becoming healthier, happier, and more whole. First, as hinted at above, our lives will never be perfect. Second, being imperfect is okay. When we realize these two things, we stop striving for an idealized version of our lives and begin, instead, to strive for the truest and best version of ourselves. Once we stop searching for 'perfect', we can even learn to move beyond the hurt, which is important because we've all been cut deeply in a variety of different ways (and, again, it's okay). Awareness is imperative in the healing process.

It is only when you are aware of your perceptions, and understand how these perceptions impact your thought patterns, that you are able to anticipate the feelings that will be conjured. You see, thoughts lead to feelings, and it is our feelings that lead to the behaviors, thereby creating a 'consequence'. Even though the word 'consequence' has a negative connotation in common usage, it simply means the result of an action. These behavioral consequences manifest into new events (or experiences to be perceived) and the cycle begins anew. Once we are able to identify and label the steps leading to each consequence and the resulting cyclical pattern in our lives then we are able to fully realize our power and that we are in control of how we respond.

Without this awareness, we will constantly operate in a reactionary mode.

We would be remiss if we didn't reiterate that this process is not an easy one and certainly not for the faint of heart. It is during the difficult and uncomfortable times when the commitment becomes an integral part of a successful change process. After we have recognized the need for change, committed to it, and started to explore the cyclical patterns that keep us trapped, it becomes necessary to examine our suffering. Even though we all experience it to some extent, this suffering is not a natural part of the human condition. Instead, suffering indicates that there is some form of imbalance or dysfunction in our lives.

For many, the dysfunction and pain are so ever-present that it is not uncommon to normalize and minimize their presence. However, whether we are ready or not, the process of making a radical change in any area of our lives will not only cause us to acknowledge the dysfunction, it will inevitably shine a spotlight on our role in creating or maintaining the dysfunction. While we may not be at fault for the initial event that triggered the suffering, we often play a part in continuing to manifest its consequences.

"I am doing it again. I'm actively planning to sabotage. It is not, at first, a conscious endeavor. I assume that my motivations are pure. But somewhere between picking up my phone, writing a seriously misguided and emotionally draining text message and pressing 'send', I catch myself and realize what I am doing. I check in with my emotions. In this moment I am exceptionally lonely. I dig deeper.

I acknowledge that my loneliness is in part fueled by the fact that I push away the people who show genuine interest in me and with whom I could form lasting human connections. I do this because I am deathly scared of heartbreak and disappointment, and I am quite aware that letting people in comes with the very real risk of both. So I trained myself to avoid the risk, indoctrinating myself with difficult messages, such as 'ignore the calls from friends reaching out because those same friends could one day turn on you'. Instead, I scroll through my phone looking to reach out to someone who can make me feel anything in this moment without fear of having my heart broken. The husband. The player. The lesbian. They are my safe haven. Because I will never give them my heart; they can never break it.

This has been 'working' for the better part of my adolescent and adult life, but why do I now feel more lonely and sad than even after a heartbreak? Maybe it is the knowledge that my desire to protect myself is jeopardizing all chances of happiness and connection. The burden of being strong and independent and the one who 'doesn't need anyone' is overwhelming right now.

I am becoming less capable of squelching the small voice inside that is telling me I need someone, that is screaming to be loved and comforted by someone other than myself. Rationally, I know that even if I am hurt, I am strong enough to survive it. But letting go and letting love in is a hurdle that I cannot seem to overcome right now even though I want to so desperately."

Awareness isn't always pleasant and the change that can be birthed from awareness isn't automatic or immediate. However, becoming aware is important and necessary in the process of growth. Once we've become aware of our patterns and determined that we don't want to be controlled by them anymore, we are able to reap the benefits of awareness.

***

Reframing

After we have recognized our patterns as the result of past insults, weaknesses and insecurities, and made a pact with ourselves to change, we are able to move confidently towards the best version of ourselves. It seems almost counterintuitive that a process so focused on change and growth can also bring acceptance. When we become aware that our 'failures' and shortcomings do not define us, but are born by our fears and insecurities, we become a lot more accepting of our emerging selves. It is then we see that our scars and the growth we have undergone as a result of these experiences are all a part of our best selves. There is often comfort found in that recognition.

"With the work I've put into myself in the past year, I am definitely the best and brightest incarnation of myself...I don't know if she will be the last 'me' that I am privileged enough to know. But she is who and where I am right now. She is loving and kind and hopeful. All things past selves weren't. And she's gentle with me."

Learning to accept where we are at this present moment is critical to our ability to move forward successfully. Once we are comfortable in naming the symptoms, we arrive at a point where we can begin to identify specific situations that lead us to these emotions.

"A few years ago I was lost. Frustrated. Scared. Unsure. Anxious. Trapped. Unfulfilled. Stuck in a dead-end job. Smothered by society's expectations. Didn't have a clue what I wanted to do with my life. I cared for myself enough to change my life, but I didn't have the slightest clue where to start. I spent my days wishing that things would change—that I could escape a life that my soul could no longer bear."

When we are able to examine the context within which these triggers, symptoms, and emotions occur, we gain (or regain) control. With this new found control, we are able to identify and articulate goals and begin devising plans to achieve our desired outcomes. Initially, setting goals sounds simple. We do it every day. We make to-do lists to help us at work or school and regularly set and achieve goals related to objective projects in our daily routines. However, when the focus shifts to our emotional or spiritual well-being, it becomes exponentially more difficult to objectify our desires and determine tangible, easily identifiable, and therefore actionable goals.

As such, setting emotional and spiritual goals may be difficult for some of us to accomplish or even fully comprehend because our emotional and spiritual well-being exists in ways that are often intangible and invisible to onlookers, and at times even to ourselves. Thus, it is important that during this process of change, the goals we set related to our emotional and spiritual well-being be those that we can identify and visualize. If we are unable to do this, then working towards them becomes an arduous and seemingly impossible task.

Take a moment and reflect on where you want to be and how you want to move through this life. If you're able to identify goals at this time, ask yourself whether they reflect an actual attainable aspiration or an overall greater state of being. The difference between the two may seem irrelevant but it makes a monumental difference.

We realize that the simple act of challenging our goals in this way may seem abstract and even confusing. However, our goals are not always clear cut; when you take a common goal like 'happiness' and start to un-package whether it is an attainable aspiration or just a general sense of being, the reason for more closely examining our goals becomes clearer. Most people search for and desperately try to obtain happiness. It is promised, explicitly or implicitly, when we buy certain products, visit exotic destinations, and experience significant and life changing events such as graduations, births and marriages. It is a concept that has been established and idealized in society, but, for most, remains vague and evades explicit definition. In fact, in our experience, the term 'happiness' is an ugly and insidious green monster that may never be reached.

The reason why is simple: happiness is not a truly attainable (or sustainable) aspiration. Happiness is a fleeting overall state of being. You will likely be happy for a moment or moments and then it will elude you again and you will find yourself returning to the exhausting search for this coveted goal. If finding happiness is your sole goal and motivation, you will likely experience a great deal of disappointment throughout your life due to its fleeting nature. You may begin to resent people who seem like they have it all and begin to feel that happiness is available to some and elusive only to you. In the age of social media, these feelings of resentment and possibly anger become even more intense given our exclusive access to the *highlight reel* of everyone's life. Seeing these snapshots of their happiness, it is easy to forget that they too have private struggles and personal tragedies that they are simply choosing not to display.

Don't misunderstand; we want you to be happy and we recognize that we all have fleeting moments of happiness. However, we also recognize that we cannot depend on these instances to sustain us. Joy, or *the emotion evoked by well-being, success, or good fortune or by the prospect of possessing what one desires,* is a much more tangible goal. We conceptualize joy as a burst of a positive energy that, most importantly, has an immediate euphoric effect on the brain. The fact that we experience the benefit of joy (e.g., dopamine release) immediately helps it to feel more tangible and achievable. Over time, as you get regular doses of joy, the overall outlook on your life will improve and you may even move closer to feeling like you've achieved happiness, but only because you've focused your attention on a tangible goal. When we establish tangible emotional goals, we can make attempts to fulfill each of them thereby achieving greater satisfaction.

If transforming your thinking were an instantaneous process, you would have already 'thought yourself happy' and erased all negative or damaging patterns simply by virtue of your desire to change. But, unfortunately the process is not that easy. In fact, there will be times when you feel like everything is against you as you undertake this transformative process. While it is highly unlikely that the universe is truly against you, it is true that life, in general, is hard. There are days when our difficulties start the moment you open your eyes in the morning. The kids will not listen. It is trash day and the garbage can sits full in the house or garage silently mocking you. The coffee creamer ran out yesterday and you forgot to replace it. You are running late. The traffic app on your phone has failed you once again and your drive to work is complete with construction zones and congestion. Your emotional responses have already escalated from mild annoyance to irritation to frustration and you've barely stepped through the doors to the office to begin your workday. As you can imagine and may have even experienced, a few more of these relatively minor instances where things do not go your way may cause you to escalate from frustration to anger and, if left unchecked, straight into crisis mode.

When this is the outlook of the day, it is near impossible to think about happiness being within your realm of control. This is one of the many reasons we acknowledged at the onset that transformation takes commitment and also why it is imperative that you slip in daily doses of fun and joy. It is helpful in the beginning to tell yourself that every day needs to have some element of joy in it. These injections of joy are essential to transforming our thinking because, frequently, we are unable to change the circumstances that we encounter. By focusing on attaining interludes of joy throughout our days, we have the power to change our outlook and regain some sense of control, even in the midst of difficult situations.

If you are like many of us who don't take time to experience joy every day (yes, even we fall into this category from time to time), don't worry. You can ease into it slowly by thinking of just five things that bring you joy. Write them down so they are tangible and you can return to the list when you are in need of a boost and forget that you have strategies in place to achieve joy. Once you've identified those five things, the next step is to determine ways to incorporate them into your routine for a minimum of ten minutes a day, because remember we want these boosts of joy to be consistent. Starting this new practice will provide its own positive emotional reinforcement and is an amazing step towards resetting our emotional triggers.

Although tempting, for this practice to be truly successful and sustainable, it is critical that these things have nothing to do with spending money and are not dependent on other people. Because reliance on material objects or other consumer goods purchased with money can quickly lead to debt or despair when we are not able to attain the object of our desire—potentially eliciting the opposite effect of joy. Avoiding reliance on other people is somewhat more nuanced. Many times we seek solace in the presence, affection, or attention of friends, family and loved ones—in fact society and our peer groups encourage this behavior. For me, my children are my greatest source of joy. Before them, I honestly never thought I was capable of feeling joy and even now when I experience it, I forget all my woes for a moment. But having your joy be contingent on someone or something else has a fatal flaw...that someone or something can (and frequently will) let you down, even unintentionally.

For example, let's say I have had a trying day at the office and I am on my way to pick up my children, full of desire and expectation to have a beautiful afternoon with them to erase all that's gone wrong with my day. As soon as we walk through the front door, before even having the chance to take off my shoes, the boys start fighting over a toy and the youngest is having a tantrum that would put the Tasmanian devil to shame...what happens to my joy then?

If we put our happiness in the hands of another to hold, they will drop it every time and our happiness and attempt at joy will be shattered or at least compromised. Please do not misunderstand our stance on the importance of friends and family. The people in our lives will of course be sources of influence for our experiences of happiness, joy and excitement; however, they should not be the ones in charge of it—that job must reside solely with you.

In addition to actively inserting these daily doses of joy into our lives, it is necessary to take a daily accounting of the positive moments that we experience organically during the day. In short, we must learn to be grateful. The research of Robert Emmons, Professor of Psychology at the University of California-Davis, on the positive implications of gratitude, suggests that, if cultivated, it has the potential to improve your health. According to Professor Emmons, gratitude has the power to "heal, energize and transform" (http://emmons.faculty.ucdavis.edu/). When we become hyper focused on all the nasty things that have happened throughout the day (and let's be honest, some days *seem* to be filled with only those things), we lose focus on the beauty around us. Losing our perspective robs us of the ability to smile, to enjoy simple things, or even to relax at the end of the night without replaying negative scripts in our head. Although it may seem an insurmountable task, being grateful is not only about the big things in life, it is about finding opportunities for gratitude even in the most mundane and ordinary aspects of our life.

Start with one thing you feel grateful for today, and each day add to your list. Ideally, each day, you will be able to come up with something, at least one thing, for which you are appreciative. In the beginning, it might be difficult to identify those things because it is not uncommon to be stuck in patterns of thinking that accentuate the negative. So, if you're having difficulty finding something today, it's okay to borrow from yesterday (or the days or weeks before), if necessary. If you are living with someone or you had a meaningful interaction with someone today, you can add what you are thankful for about that person or interaction. I originally started this exercise with my son, who was four at the time. Our goal was to express one thing we were grateful for each day throughout the entire month of Thanksgiving (November) without any repeats. This practice can be encouraging; it can remind us that even in the midst of chaos, there is still positivity.

Now, in this world of constant social media updates from everyone from old classmates to celebrities, you can witness people's expressions of gratitude year round. And although we are often happy for them, if you have not cultivated a practice of finding things in your life for which you are grateful, looking at other people's expressions of gratitude might actually feel stressful or upsetting and return you to those feelings of resentment and anger. Again, this is about perspective. Try to avoid spending significant amounts of time and energy focusing on what they claim to have that you do not. Focus instead on what you have that is uniquely yours and avoid the trap of comparison.

"Periodically, I find myself having to take breaks from both social media and social reality (e.g., reality television). These breaks almost always come about in the same way... There is a lull or some kind of stagnation in my life that leads me to feel like something is missing and I need to reconnect with someone or something. Instead of turning my focus within and trying to regain a sense of balance and focus on my practice of gratitude, I externalize and look to the outside for clues to what I may be missing. I don't think I do it consciously. I never go on Facebook with the stated intention to troll newsfeeds for evidence of what might be missing in my own life. Nor do I turn on reality shows

where stars flaunt their fabulous lives thinking 'let's see if I can identify where I went wrong'. But somehow, in the hours spent lost in these alternative realities (ones in which, admittedly, I am seeing only a small glimpse into what people's lives and experiences are really like), I start to develop these nagging feelings of self-doubt and longing. I find myself feeling sad because I didn't have a huge wedding with a princess dress and hundreds of guests. Because I'm not married with 2.5 kids, picket fence, and dog. Because my summer vacation didn't include yacht rides or cocktail parties. Just because...I feel sad until I realize that these are not even my goals. When I realize that I have fallen into the dangerous game of comparison and am being tormented by what society says I should want and don't have, I know that it is time to take a break. Go offline, unplug the TV, and avoid the tabloids in the grocery aisles. It is time to remember that I have goals for myself and that I should be and truly am thankful that my life is bringing me closer to achieving them (even if that progress is painfully slow)."

Because many of us have lived our lives with the task of getting from one accomplishment to the next or simply surviving the day, the practice of focusing on gratitude may seem foreign. We may even find that it is not so easy to just start naming the good things in our lives. I know that personally coming up with lists during those early days was challenging, which was especially true if I was having a bad day. I soon realized, however, that no matter what was going on in my life—business problems, illness (myself or others), someone cut me off in traffic, uncooperative kids, car trouble—there was ALWAYS something for which I could be grateful. Your list doesn't have to be complex; in fact, my early lists were quite simple.

- My health—which at times could be better but I have learned to be thankful nonetheless,
- The smile on my babies' faces,
- A business that, for the most part, is thriving and that I can be proud to call my own,
- A home,

- A partner to come home and talk to,
- A car to drive,
- Money to eat out.

Keep in mind this is not my original list…as I mentioned, in the beginning it was much shorter (with only one or two items on occasion).

In a 2003 study, *Counting Blessings Versus Burdens: An Experimental Investigation of Gratitude and Subjective Well-Being in Daily Life*, Robert A. Emmons and Michael E. McCullough asked participants to write a few sentences each week, focusing on pre-specified topics. The participants were split into three groups. The first group wrote about things they were grateful for, the second group wrote about daily irritations or things that had displeased them, and the third group simply wrote about events that had affected them (with no emphasis on the positive or negative). After 10 weeks, the first group, those who wrote about gratitude, were more optimistic and felt better about their lives.

Finding things to be grateful for doesn't mean that everything is perfect. In fact, often times our biggest lessons in gratitude come when we begin to examine instances in our lives where we have a choice to be defeated or to grow. In our personal experience, we have found that sometimes when you weather the storm and find that after the clouds have cleared you are still standing, there is more to be grateful for than in those instances when you avoided the storms of life all together.

"I still have a hard time naming my emotions. After 35 plus years of ignoring my feelings or trying to suppress them when ignoring has failed, I sometimes find myself sitting, speechless, lost in 'feeling'. Today, during one of those times, it came to me that I feel thankful. I don't think that's an emotion, but it is what I feel.

Yesterday, I had the biggest health scare of my life. But today I find myself beyond the fear of dying from the same potentially preventable condition that claimed the lives of both my grandmother and my brother. I am totally over the fleeting anger

34

at the universe for the next eight months of twice daily injections. And I have somehow managed to avoid the unspoken tirade against myself for not pursuing genetic testing which could have potentially saved me from this current diagnosis or at least prepared me for it. It is so amazing to me that after realizing all of what I don't feel, I am left with the aforementioned sense of thankfulness. I am not dead. I noticed the symptoms and pursued medical treatment before an everyday blood clot traveled somewhere in my body that would have translated to irreparable damage or death. I have amazing health insurance. I came in contact with a tremendous medical team that was able to test, diagnose, and get me started on treatment within six hours. I now have a deeper and more profound sense of empathy for the millions of people suffering from life altering chronic conditions.

In this moment, I am thankful for what I have gained throughout this process, instead of what I have lost or the ways in which this will disrupt my lifestyle. Maybe most importantly, I learned that there is an incrementally small thing that changes an event from chaos to crisis—your attitude. The same exact event that in the past would have sent me into a tailspin of negative emotions became instead an opportunity for me to reflect. I once scoffed at 'reframing' for being inadequate to help deal with what seemed like insurmountable troubles. After this experience. I see it as a tool that allows you to navigate through life's chaos without getting sucked into crisis mode. It isn't perfect of course and has its limits (even as a believer in its usefulness, I still wouldn't suggest this to my friend who has a four year old battling cancer). I know that reframing will not completely alleviate a real crisis. I will, however, say that in the words of one of my favorite artists, 'there's a blessing in every lesson', and sometimes focusing on that is enough to keep your head above water."

Pieces of Me, Ledisi

People just don't know what I'm about
They haven't seen what's there behind my smile
There's so much more of me I'm showing now
(These are the pieces of me)

When it looks like I'm up, sometimes I'm down
I'm alone even with people all around
But that don't change the happiness I found
(These are the pieces of me)

So when you look at my face
You gotta know that I'm made
Of everything love and pain
These are the pieces of me

3. Norming
Who Am I and Why Am I Important?

To navigate this life successfully, it is imperative that you know who you truly are. In order to arrive at an understanding of your true self, you must *explore* what makes you undeniably *you*. In developing this sense of self, you will think about all aspects of your magnificent and multifaceted self. This is the time to explore your past, your fears and your desires. It seems so cliché, but I am reminded of the saying "if you don't know what you stand for you will fall for anything." If we want to stand strong against the storms of life, we have to know who we are and remain grounded by tapping into that sense of self daily. You must build an unshakable foundation, which serves as the core of who you are—a secure sense of self.

Having a secure sense of self is about more than just who you perceive yourself to be and how you develop and act on your values. It also represents how you interact with the world, including how you maintain your social support networks and your coping skills. Your sense of self is what roots you to this world and keeps you grounded so you are not blown away or destroyed in the storm. This process is worthwhile given that the core of who you are does not change. Once you understand yourself, your understanding will continue to grow, mature and manifest accordingly depending on your life experiences.

The journey to figuring out who you are has a lot to do with tapping into your intuition. Because, the core of who you are has already been developed at some earlier stage in life; it doesn't change. Keeping that in mind somewhere, intuitively, you have the answers to all the questions you need to come face-to-face with your truest self. For some, this process may be easy, but for most it will require some reflection and conscious attempts to quiet the internal chatter and negative thoughts that keep us from recognizing ourselves. Many of us move through life with ideas about ourselves that have been handed to us by those who may only have a passing knowledge of who we are. Unfortunately, our attempts to form these definitions for ourselves and independent of the opinions of outside observers are somewhat infrequent. When we do, we may be stunted in our attempts by our lack of experience being truly honest with ourselves.

When you're ready, take a moment and finish the statements below. This will come as close to 'free association' as we will ask you to do in this book. Don't think about it; just respond with the first thought that comes to mind, write it down, and move on to the next statement. At this point, do not attempt to make sense of the statements, your responses, or the implications. (Trust us, that's a can of worms you don't want to open right now, but we'll get there!!!) Think of this as a piece of art; let your intuition lead you and believe that the 'work' will take shape. Only once it has fully formed can meaning be assigned.

Defining Self

Statements of Self-Description

- I am a person who…
- All of my life…
- Ever since I was child…
- One of the things I feel proud of…
- It's hard for me to admit…
- One of the things I can't forgive is…
- One of the things I feel guilty about is…
- If I didn't have to worry about my image…
- One of the ways people hurt me is…
- Mother was always…
- What I needed from mother but didn't get was…
- Father was always…
- What I needed from father but didn't get was…

- If I weren't afraid to be myself, I might…
- One of the things I'm angry about is…
- What I need and have never received from a woman
- What I need and have never received from a man is
- The bad thing about growing up is…
- One of the ways I could help myself but don't is to…

We realize that these statements may seem completely random and may even appear unrelated to figuring out who you are. However, if you look closely, your answers reveal a pattern of values and triggers. Your responses to these statements will identify what you hold dear. For example, I am a person who enjoys deep conversations. This truth reveals my desire for emotional intimacy and authenticity with those whom I choose to devote my time—this includes my patients, friends, significant others, and family. It furthermore reveals this as a trigger. I am offended by pretentious people as well as by those who lack the willingness or capacity to hold intellectual or otherwise meaningful conversations.

Right now you may be wondering why this is important. The explanation is quite simple. If we are not aware of our values and triggers, we go through life reacting to what the world throws our way instead of being able to operate proactively and navigate our own paths. When we lack awareness, we are easily manipulated by our circumstances. Conversely, by having an awareness of the things that set us off, we are able to better respond to our surroundings instead of simply reacting to the situations we face.

Awareness allows us to be in full control of our thoughts. And since, as we have learned, our thoughts lead to feelings which then motivate our behaviors—ultimately resulting in a consequence, whether positive or negative—awareness is critical. You see, it is only through self-awareness, that we can begin to write the future we want for ourselves. Carl Jung summarizes this eloquently with the simple statement "Until you make the unconscious conscious, it will direct your life and you will call it fate."

"Loss has so many faces: betrayal, heartbreak, death, doubt or disappointment. Each person based on their past experiences will define what loss means differently. For me, I feel uncertainty is the hardest pill to swallow. It is doubt and uncertainty that bleeds into my sense of safety. It is like spilled black ink and its tentacles spread like wisps of smoke choking the breath I have left to survive. You see, I find solace and security in the comfort of what is known and what is in my realm of control. By this I do not mean that I need to be in charge of everything, I just mean that I need to see where I am headed next. It's funny, really, I was at the precipice of the water slide recently. This massive tunnel dropping who knows how many feet into the darkness and who knows where it would land, and all I could think of was I need to see where I am going. If my back is turned, the anxiety will overwhelm me, while if I can face the challenge, I will be okay. This is not the only incident. I remember being in Mexico and during the hike through the forest and zip lining over the lake, I was my true self: curious, mischievous, daring and alive. Until we came up to the mouth of a cave. It was not the cave that was haunting; it was the fact that I would be lowered into it using a pulley system...backwards. Yup, I needed to lean back and fall back so the experienced guide could lower me in. I had watched plenty of people do it; I knew it was safe (cognitively), but my heart couldn't let go. I couldn't let go. Oh, I used all of my skills at charming these fellows to please let me come on the other side so that I could lean forward;, I tried to convince them that I could just jump the 200 feet into the cave filled with water, and even proposed that I just use the rope and climb down? Was it really just an issue of control over the unknown or was it something more?

I learned early on that the world is not safe and people will not be kind. Physical pain does not hold a candle to the mental anguish and torture of how will tomorrow be? I learned that the people I love and who are supposed to love me back, may not be there when I wake up in the morning. I learned that there is no such thing as unconditional love. I learned that just when you think they couldn't really say something so cruel...they do. When lessons like these are learned at such an early age, your view on the human condition creates certain deeply ingrained values that you begin to hold dear. For me, those values are safety, honesty, freedom, independence, loyalty, security, self-control, hope, commitment, being loved, passion, dependability, accountability, and openness, just to name a few. As finding people who mirror these values can bring about immense feelings of joy and peace; those who violate these will bring about despondence and a sense of loss. This loss can manifest in feelings of betrayal, heartache, or doubt in oneself.

It is when my values are violated, that those nasty self-deprecating messages come back to the surface: 'You are not worth loving; why wouldn't he do **that**? You think you are so smart and look, it's the same thing again, you idiot. People might think you're pretty, but they'll never love you. Get out of my sight; you are worthless. It's not you I wanted; it's the potential of what you would become. You're not worth the hassle of protecting. You're not worth the risk.' I believed all of these to be true and for a long time, this is exactly what I got back from the universe; a sea of people who reinforced the beliefs I had as a result of the messages I had received whether overtly, or implicitly. This pattern continued until I had had enough. There were really only two ways out of this for me: either to take my life and affirm that these messages are true, or to tell the world I had manifested to 'go fuck itself'. I chose the latter and it still took a long time to finally find my worth. I found it through my passions and the family I created for myself.

I wish I could say that these demons no longer surface; they do, in the form of uncertainty. Whether it's a new adventure, a new relationship, a new business venture, or a new client. I've learned that any time I doubt myself, my abilities, or the intentions of another, I set myself up to fight these messages again. What to do? I take charge. I force that sense of safety through knowledge. Knowledge of what's to come and for what I should be prepared. Through open communication, and a thorough plan that may be ever changing. I seek support from my people; those who have lasted the test of time and have proven their love and loyalty. I take control. I take the power

41

back from my past messages and I challenge them. And, in doing so, I take that first apprehensive, but determined, step forward."

***

Value Development

Using the themes from the previous section, let's elaborate and try to pinpoint specific values. Put simply, your values reflect what is important to you—who you are, what you hold dear, what upsets you, and what underlies your decisions are all connected to your personal values. They are a shorthand way of describing your motivations. Together with your beliefs, your values are the causal factors that drive your decision-making. The whole point of discovering your values is to improve the results you get in those areas that truly are most important to you. Values act as our compass; they put us back on course every single day helping to ensure that we are moving in the direction that takes us closer and closer to our definition of the best life we could possibly live.

To make this process simpler, I have included a list for you to review and select from *The Prime Solutions Participant Workbook*. I would like you, first, to categorize these values into the following three sections: (1) Very Important, (2) Important, and (3) Not Important. After you have completed the first step of the process, step two is to organize the values within each of the three categories by their order of importance. For example, if romance, forgiveness, and money are all in your 'very important' category, which among these would you say you value the most? Second? Third?

Skill	Attractiveness	Popularity
God's Will	Flexibility	Fun
Money	Generosity	Appearance
Hope	Caring	Influence
Romance	Forgiveness	Sexuality
Fitness	Self-control	Fairness
Purpose	Challenge	Achievement
Stability	Growth	Creativity
Self-respect	Commitment	Family
Risk	Excitement	Loving
Faithfulness	Self-Esteem	Passion
Safety	Health	Being Loved
Helpfulness	Acceptance	Intimacy
Openness	Friendship	Learning
Independence	Spirituality	Tradition
Inner Peace	Honesty	Freedom
Responsibility	Courtesy	Simplicity
Accountability	Laughter	Protection
Quality Time	Dependability	Open-minded

Okay, now that you have arranged these values in order of personal importance, we will focus on the top five values in each category. Don't worry if a category has fewer than five values in it; just work with what is there. The following are a few questions for you to ask yourself about those high priority values:

1. Why is this value important to me?
2. What are some of the things that I do to protect these values?
3. In what ways are these values influenced by family, personal experiences, or my cultural heritage?
4. What am I doing to live up to these values?
5. How do these values fit with changes I want to make in my life?
6. How do these values fit with my goals?

By consciously prioritizing your values, you will be able to rely on them when you need to make important decisions in the future. For example, if you know that what you value most in life is to experience inner peace, then when you are presented with propositions or opportunities that are contrary to your ability to achieve inner peace, it will be easier for you to say no. Knowing that you are standing up for yourself or your personal values when you make decisions that may upset others can help you stick to them with a sense of conviction that you otherwise wouldn't have.

If I were to ask you to tell me who you are, how would you describe yourself? Many people can list off generic responses they've practiced or have possibly learned about themselves through past experiences. Common responses include descriptors like intelligent, funny, or open-minded. However, we believe that individuals are more than a list of adjectives. If I was presented with a folder containing 20 forms filled out by 20 different people, all describing themselves, how would I know which description was yours? Of course we all share some universal qualities; however, we are all unique and intriguing within ourselves—and, those are the components of 'you' that will differentiate you from the other 19 pages in the folder.

In this moment, I would like you to consider what makes you who you are without using those 'go to' defining characteristics. Much like we delved deeper into our desire to love and be loved and found, that at the root of our desire, we are often looking for acceptance, companionship or some other feeling that we have associated with 'love'. So, take a moment now to go deeper than your generic descriptors. Look within your soul, where the truth of your unique existence lies, mostly dormant, and bring it to light. Allow it to flow from deep within your consciousness, as an artist would if he were to fully give in to his craft. Look to the themes and values from our previous work and use them as your guide in painting this picture of your unique self. Much like in other activities, take this time to articulate what you feel without allowing the internal filter to edit your thoughts. Just write. There are no wrong answers. There are no consequences.

> *"I am the sounds of the piano, playing softly and smoothly. I am the smile and joy in my students' faces. I am at times a warm spring afternoon, and at others a cold winter by the fire. I am the blue Grecian water that feels different than it looks. I am a snake that slithers by you without a sound. I am the hurts of my past and the hope of my future. I am the sound of feet running against the pavement."*
> —*Kaitlyn D.*

***

Value Development

The second stage is where we truly begin to process. This is where we start to unearth patterns of behavior, recognize and become aware of...*something.* This stage is the beginning of mindfulness—the practice of paying attention. It is important that we are paying attention since internal discord and its behavioral manifestations do not occur randomly; rather, they follow distinctive and systematic patterns. Repetitions are the simplest patterns, and they are easily identified by their inadequate presentation. When we speak of the inadequate presentation of these patterns, we mean that there are no apparent external factors that serve as triggers and no obvious associative link with the general context of the situation. When such a pattern occurs regularly, the identification of the common elements in the situations provides the first clues as to its meaning.

Although there are similarities, the manifestations of our insecurities will not appear the same for everyone or even for us across time. However, the underlying motive can often be tied back to an integral fear within us. In order to identify the root of this fear, we must engage in a process of self-reflection; because often, the common element is so deeply embedded in your unconscious that it isn't readily visible to you or those around you. As Carl Jung stated, "until you make the unconscious conscious, it will direct your life and you will call it fate".

"It was the spring of my senior year in high school, I was on the phone with my then boyfriend (later fiancé), and as had become the norm, I was upset about something. Undoubtedly, I was making the same self-deprecating comments that, by then, had become a constant part of my lexicon. He listened politely for as long as he could before he interrupted me and made what, at that time in my life was, the most powerful statement I had ever heard: 'I shouldn't love you more than you love yourself.'

I remember that—even in my state of unawareness—the comment touched something in me that I thought I had hidden very carefully away, behind all of my bravado and sass. I did not love myself. Somewhere along the way, the confidence of childhood had been stripped away. I had been broken and violated and abandoned, from which I inferred that I was unlovable and unworthy. So, I craved love, attention, and validation from those around me; because if they could love me, maybe I wasn't as unlovable as I thought—and maybe their love for me would begin to shed light on those dark places that I had hidden away until I felt whole again.

It is for this reason that at 36 I have not had a single successful relationship. It is my motivation for creating conflict when there is none just to see if they'll stay through the difficult times. It is my reason for needing to be 'chosen' over their other lovers and friends. My relationships haven't worked because I've never really been looking for a lover; every time I've ventured to let someone close, I have been looking for a savior, and as soon as I get the inclination that their love or whatever it is that they are offering is insufficient to heal me, I run. By running I don't mean that I leave; quite the opposite actually. I dig my heels in and show that I am rooted right where I am in an effort to demonstrate my commitment and then I show them the very ugliest parts of myself. Some of them I even exaggerate for affect.

I become mean spirited and negative. I am critical about their weaknesses and broken parts. Eventually they leave because every ounce of energy I put into the universe is filled with anger and pain and leaving is the inevitable result. But the irony of the whole thing is that I then use their leaving as evidence of my earlier assessment of myself. The message that I hear and see is that I am unlovable and unworthy.

It has only been recently that I understood the part I played in this whole 20 year dating debacle, and the realization only came after I started exploring those hidden, implicit, underlying beliefs through therapy. It hurts like hell to admit that you don't love yourself. I feel like a failure every time I think about it. Some days I feel no connection with myself and these are the times when I feel most alone, even in a crowd. I still desperately want someone to reach in and love me beyond this feeling but I know that no one besides me is capable of that. I am the only one that can save me. I know now that until I stop looking for saviors, I will never truly have the love I desire."

***

Need Fulfillment

In our modern Western world, when discussions turn to the concept of *need,* our minds, almost instinctively, begin to quickly flip through an invisible catalog of all the things we 'need'. Many of these so called needs are modern conveniences that generations past have lived quite fulfilling lives without having. Thus, the Kate Spade handbag, Armani suit, and trips abroad are not what we are referring to when we bring up the concept of need. Instead, when we talk about *human need* we are talking about something much more basic, almost primal.

Human needs are a powerful source of explanation for human behavior and social interaction. They include both physical and nonphysical elements needed for human growth and development, as well as all those things humans are innately driven to attain. If you examine the formation of your values, it may become obvious that they are often a result of important needs that were either met or not met during our early formative years, from birth to age eight. Understanding these needs, and which ones you are trying to meet in any given moment, can help you create new patterns that may actually lead to lasting fulfillment, instead of temporary satisfaction.

In 1943, Abraham Maslow explored these basic human needs in his book <u>Motivation and Personality</u>. As a result of his exploration, he developed a powerful theory about the existence of human needs, specifically that they fit into one of several categories and can be ordered hierarchically. What has now been termed *Maslow's Hierarchy of Needs* is most frequently displayed as a pyramid with five levels (as seen below). At the bottom of the pyramid, we see the physiological need for food and shelter—our most basic and primitive need—followed by the need for safety, the need to belong or be loved, the need for power and control, and finally, at the top, the need for self-actualization and fulfillment. Based on this theory, individuals start out trying to fulfill their most basic needs and move up the hierarchy in an attempt to fulfill increasingly complex needs as each of the preceding needs are satisfied.

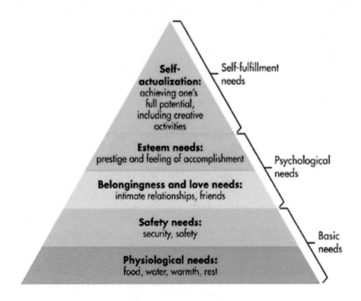

The needs at the bottom of the pyramid are basic physical requirements including the need for food, water, sleep, and warmth. Without these, it is difficult for people to think about achieving anything else because these needs are essential to survival. If you can imagine someone on their last leg as it relates to survival, for example, having been without water for several days, then finding water and sustenance becomes their primary concern. In this instance, an individual will likely be unable to accomplish or even acknowledge higher level needs.

Physical safety, an essential basic human need, will not become a priority until they have satisfied their quest for water because, without it, they will surely perish—thus survival is prioritized above safety. Once these lower-level needs have been met, the overwhelming instinct to survive quiets (unless another threat to basic physical survival arises) and individuals can move on to the next level of needs—safety and security.

The desire for things such as security, order, law, stability, and freedom from fear are all potential components of our safety needs. If these important needs are not met, for example, in countries experiencing war and internal strife, an individual's primary focus will be on survival with the goal of just getting through that moment or that day. Self-preservation becomes paramount and the individual is unlikely to be able to focus on anything other than survival. Although Maslow's theory included only physical safety, in my years as a therapist, I have learned to also include emotional safety at this level of the hierarchy. For our purposes, emotional safety is defined as the ability to be vulnerable and exposed without being met with a consequence. This sense of emotional safety is essential and is therefore the first important goal that I strive to reach with the people I work with; it is how we develop trust and emotional intimacy.

Although we feel emotionally safe when we are in nurturing environments, true emotional safety comes from within. It is the 'knowing' part of what we are feeling; the ability to identify our feelings and then take the ultimate risk of actually allowing ourselves to experience them. Granted, given our varied experiences with war, trauma, childhood abuse, neglect, and other forms of violence or victimization, it is possible that some of us have never experienced the manifestation of emotional safety. Because it may be absolutely foreign to us, we may come to believe that safety is all an illusion, based on fiction, possibly experienced by 'others' but wholly unrealistic and beyond our grasp. If we cannot even fathom the possibility of physical and emotional safety as a reality in our lives, we will not be able to fulfill these needs. This, unfortunately, leaves us stuck, unable to move beyond this level of the hierarchy.

If we are lucky enough to experience physical and emotional safety, we are able to move beyond a desire to simply survive and on to the third of Maslow's levels—love and belonging. This may be the first of Maslow's levels to truly resonate with some. Depending on your life circumstances you may or may not have experienced a conscious struggle to have your more basic needs met; however, most of us are consciously aware of trying to fulfill this need for love and belonging. We satisfy this need in a number of ways including relationships with caring, compassionate, and empathetic individuals; developing a sense of place or belonging in our social world; being part of a community where we feel accepted and approved of; or love in the more traditional sense of attention and physical affection. Upon successfully obtaining the type of love necessary to fulfill this level of the hierarchy, you may have experienced and will more fully understand the importance of finding a sense of acceptance and emotional intimacy solely on the basis of who you are, and not who someone else wants you to be. This stage is integral to mastering our acceptance of self.

The fourth level of Maslow's Hierarchy is power and control. Although attractive, this level is not about experiencing the 'I rule you! You will succumb to my power!' type of control. The power that we speak of is based, instead, in a feeling of having autonomy—a sense of freedom and independence in which you feel that you have some say over the direction in your life on a day to day basis. Imagine a scenario where a child has grown up in a familial and social environment where their existence has been wrought with rejection, ridicule and constant messages of being a burden, unworthy or inconvenient. As a result of not being fully accepted or integrated into the family or other social settings, the child (and the subsequent adult) is unlikely to feel like their needs are being taken into consideration in even the most routine situations. Studies have repeatedly shown that these individuals are more socially withdrawn, depressed, insecure, and much more likely to engage in behavior that puts their safety at risk.

It may be difficult for individuals who do not feel accepted or loved to believe they are valued and important. Without feeling that you are of value or that the role you fulfill in family or society is important, it is difficult for individuals to experience 'success' at this level of the hierarchy. When this level has been achieved, however, individuals may experience feelings of achievement, mastery, independence, status, dominance, prestige, respect from others and, possibly most important of all, self-respect.

"You meet after so many years and it is as if nothing has changed, yet everything is different. His smile, the way he looks

at me, the kindness in his words and gestures. You wonder just how much this man has grown since the last encounter. He was eager to be with me, to get to know and understand me. He adores me. He would take time and drive 30 minutes to me and back just to have 15 minutes of my company. I am completely enamored with him. I think to myself, 'Wow! The universe is finally sending me someone who will love me back the way I will love them.'

We spent hours on the phone discussing life, hopes, theories, family systems, education and the news and religion... it seemed as though no topics were off limits to explore. I loved his mouth. Kissing him, I would find myself lost in his arms. The entire world around me would fall away and it was just us. He is thoughtful, kind, and loving effortlessly. He shares his knowledge and expertise and soaks up all of mine. There was no consequence to what I would share with him and most certainly none from me. He made me feel safe emotionally. He shared his history of how he had defended his friends and even ex-girlfriends in sketchy situations so I felt physically safe with him as well. Knight in shining armor couldn't begin to describe the way he pampered me...Being with him, near him, growing with him, I felt safety, love, belonging, and acceptance.

So what happened? Time was no longer worth spending when it didn't benefit him. I was left questioning where he was and what happened when dinner plans were ignored. I would sit there and wait and wait and think to myself over and over, something must have happened. Then I would get a text or call to cancel and a small piece of my heart would chip away. The man who would travel for an hour to have 15 minutes with me, started to forget to check on me while I was ill and would make other plans. Slowly, the hopes I had begun to fade. The man who once serenaded me with beautiful words of affirmation had started to criticize and put me down—first by dismissing my opinions and then escalating to personal assaults on my character and personality. What happened? I began to wonder if I had dreamt it all up.

Any time I would bring up my concerns, he would say I am reading too much into it and I am making a big deal out of nothing. I felt I was losing my sense of power and control over the course of my life. I thought we were living parallel lives...and then it slowly turned around. What happened? We had built his beautiful life and it was unraveling...what happened? I no longer felt secure. I didn't feel emotionally safe. I didn't feel love and belonging and certainly not accepted. I was too passionate, too sensitive, too rigid or cold, too naïve, too skeptical, too carefree...I wasn't good enough. I couldn't win no matter which way I chose to behave. I started walking around planning how to present thoughts and plans. I slowly began to lose myself so I could keep him.

By the end of this dysfunctional dance, I had once again lost all that made me, me. I learned once again that if you put your happiness in someone else's hands, they'll drop it. They will drop it every time."

For some, the process of achieving the first four needs in Maslow's Hierarchy can take a lifetime. Some people, especially those in environments that are inherently unsafe or who struggle with financial security, may be stuck in a mode of constantly trying to obtain sufficient resources to meet their physiological needs. Others, like the child who has been repeatedly berated, may be battling their own internal shadows to come to a place of feeling power and control. We all stumble along the way to realizing these needs and shouldn't beat ourselves up when this occurs. Keep in mind that the life we lead is not singular or linear when it comes to meeting needs or setting goals. We will hit roadblocks and face setbacks that will kick us all the way down to the physical or emotional safety stage and we must then work using the skills we have learned thus far to cope, process, reframe and work our way back up the stages.

***

Defense Mechanisms – For Better or Worse

So far, in this section, we have focused on mindfulness and the learning to identify our processes of coping when things do not go our way. These are our defense mechanisms, ways we have learned to adapt and get past the situation and survive. Although they sometimes get a bad rap, they are a necessary part of our everyday life. They serve to protect us from the nervousness (anxiety) that threatens to expose our weaknesses. They manifest through the manners in which we behave or think in certain ways to better protect or 'defend' ourselves.

For most of my life, there have been memories I simply could not access. I didn't have amnesia, at least not in the traditional sense, but there have been holes in my memory that made no sense to me. Things I felt without knowing the cause, like my distrust of men and feelings of voicelessness. I don't think the memories associated with trauma are ever really lost, more like repressed. I have always KNOWN, from a place where I exist only as feeling and not thought or rationalization, that I was molested.

Because I had no memory of it, I've often thought I had imagined something or maybe confused someone's story with my own. I would often tell myself I was overreacting when I wouldn't let boyfriends touch me, when I perceived my dad's inability to keep me safe or when I felt small, powerless and without voice. But whether I was overreacting or not, that became my frame, and every time I reacted in a way that was consistent with someone who had been sexually victimized, I felt reassured that I wasn't crazy for how I felt. Yet and still, after 30 years of seeking, I only had one counselor who, like me, acknowledged my trauma history without requiring me to be able to provide evidence or at least a plausible story for what had happened.

It was a relief to have someone believe me without caveats. I think it may have been her trust in me and my experience and her willingness to accept all of it and protect me as much as possible that allowed the memory to finally reveal itself to me. It happened all at once, like a flood. One minute I was at rest, concentrating on my breathing and the next, the memory was just there, in its totality, no longer begging to be recognized or given voice but simply existing as my truth.

Do you see patterns in behavior that resemble defense mechanisms? Don't worry if you can't recognize them at first; many of our defense mechanisms are unconscious and we typically don't realize that we are using them in the moment. We don't consciously call upon our ability to intellectualize, deflect, or rationalize. We just do it. Although defense mechanisms have their purpose and utility in our daily lives, it is important to be cognizant of when we are using them and to utilize approaches that are healthy. When we allow ourselves to operate from a place of fear and in a manner that is purely reactionary, we run the risk of isolating others, damaging relationships and closing ourselves off to beautiful possibilities. Dr. Susan Krauss Whitbourne outlines some of the most common defense mechanisms, and we have included them here:

> ***Denial.*** *You can consider this the 'generic' defense mechanism because it underlies many of the others. When you use denial, you simply refuse to accept the truth or reality of a fact or experience. 'No, I'm just a social smoker', is a good example; similarly people can apply this to any bad habit they wish to distance themselves from including excessive alcohol or substance use, compulsive shopping or gambling, and the like. 'Just say no', in this case means that you protect your self-esteem by failing to acknowledge your own behavior. Denial may also be used by victims of trauma or disasters and it may, at times, be a beneficial initial protective response. In the long run, however, denial can prevent you from incorporating unpleasant information about yourself and your life and have potentially destructive consequences.*

> ***Repression.*** *One step above denial in the generic classification scheme, repression involves simply*

forgetting something bad. You might forget an unpleasant experience, in the past, such as a car accident at which you were found to be at fault. You might (also experience manifestations of) repression when you 'forget' to do something unpleasant such as seeing the dentist or meeting with an acquaintance you don't really like. Repression, like denial, can be temporarily beneficial, particularly if you've forgotten something bad that happened to you, but as with denial, if you don't come to grips with the experience, it may come back to haunt you.

Regression. *From repression to regression—one little 'g' makes all the difference. In regression, you revert to a childlike emotional state in which your unconscious fears, anxieties, and general 'angst' reappear. In Freud's theory of 'psychosexual' development, people develop through stages such as the oral, anal, and phallic so that by the time they're five or six, the basic structures of personality are laid down. However, every once in a while, a person reverts to a childlike state of development, particularly under conditions of stress. The road rage you see when drivers are stuck in traffic is a great example of regression. People may also show regression when they return to a child-like state of dependency. Retreating under the blankets when you've had a bad day is one possible instance. The problem with regression is that you may regret letting your childish-self show in a self-destructive way. Driving badly or refusing to talk to people who've made you feel bad, mad, or sad can eventually get you in worse trouble than what you had when you began.*

Displacement. *In displacement, you transfer your original feelings that would get you in trouble* *(usually anger) away from the person who is the target of your rage to a more hapless and harmless victim. Here's the classic example: You've had a very unpleasant interaction with your boss or teacher, but you can't show your anger toward him or her. Instead, you come home and, so to speak, 'kick the cat' (or dog). That's not very nice imagery, but you get the picture. Any time you shift your true feelings from their original, anxiety-provoking source to one you perceive as less likely to cause you harm, you're quite possibly using displacement. Unfortunately, displacement may protect you from being fired or failing a class, but it won't protect your hand if you decide to displace your anger from the true target to a window or wall.*

Projection. *The first four defense mechanisms were relatively easy to understand, I think. Projection is more challenging. First, you have to start with the assumption that to recognize a particular quality in yourself would cause you psychic pain. Let's take a kind of silly example. For instance, you feel that an outfit you spent too much on looks really bad on you. Wearing this outfit, you walk into the room where, in your opinion, your friends stare at you perhaps for a moment too long. They say nothing and do nothing that in reality could be construed as critical. However, your insecurity about the outfit (and distress at having paid too much for it) leads you to 'project' your feelings onto your friends, and you blurt out 'Why are you looking at me like that? Don't you like this outfit?' See how silly that was? In a less silly case, you might project your more general feelings of guilt or insecurity onto friends— or worse—people who don't know and love you with all your projected flaws. Let's say you're worried that you're not really very smart. You make a dumb mistake that no one says anything about at all, and* accuse others of saying that you're dumb, inferior, or just plain stupid. The point is that no one said anything that in reality could be construed as critical. You are 'projecting' your insecurities onto others and in the process, alienating them (and probably looking somewhat foolish, as well).

Reaction formation. Now we're getting into advanced defense mechanism territory. Most people have difficulty understanding reaction formation, but it's really quite straightforward. Let's say that you secretly harbor lustful feelings towards someone from whom you should probably stay away. You don't want to admit to these feelings, so you instead express the very opposite of those feelings. This object of your lust now becomes the object of your bitter hatred. This defense mechanism could be subtitled the 'lady doth protest too much', that wonderful quote from Hamlet. A less highbrow example is 'Church Lady', the old Dana Carvey character from Saturday Night Live. Her secret obsession with pornography became reversed into her extreme scorn for all things sexual. In short, reaction formation means expressing the opposite of your inner feelings in your outward behavior.

Intellectualization. You might also neutralize your feelings of anxiety, anger, or insecurity in a way that is less likely to lead to embarrassing moments than some of the above defense mechanisms. In intellectualization, you think away an emotion or reaction that you don't enjoy feeling. For instance, rather than confront the intense distress and rejection you feel after your roommate suddenly decides to move out, you conduct a detailed financial analysis of how much you can afford to spend now that you're on your own. Although you *aren't denying that the event occurred, you're not thinking about its emotional consequences.*

Rationalization. *When you rationalize something, you try to explain it away. As a defense mechanism, rationalization is somewhat like intellectualization, but it involves dealing with a piece of bad behavior on your part rather than converting a painful or negative emotion into a more neutral set of thoughts. People often use rationalization to shore up their insecurities or remorse after doing something they regret such as an 'oops' moment. It's easier to blame someone else than to take the heat yourself, particularly if you would otherwise feel shame or embarrassment. For example, let's say you lose your temper in front of people you want to like and respect you. Now, to help make yourself feel better, you mentally attribute your outburst to a situation outside your control, and twist things so that you can blame someone else for provoking you.*

Sublimation. *We've just seen that people can use their emotions to fire up a cognitively-oriented response. Intellectualization tends to occur over the short run, but sublimation develops over a long period of time, perhaps even throughout the course of a person's career. A classic example is that of a surgeon who takes hostile impulses and converts them into 'cutting' other people in a way that is perfectly acceptable in society. This is perhaps putting things in terms that are too extreme. More realistically, sublimation occurs when people transform their conflicted emotions into productive outlets. They do say that psychologists are inherently nosy (not true!!), but it's possible that people who go into human services fields to help others are trying to 'pay forward' to compensate for difficulties they experienced in their early lives.*

As we can see, even though defense mechanisms can be adaptive and allow us to function in uncomfortable situations, they can also be unhealthy. The greatest problems arise when defense mechanisms are overused in order to avoid dealing with problems. Our goal here is to uncover these unconscious defense mechanisms and find better, healthier ways of coping with anxiety and distress.

> *"I am not what happened to me,*
> *I am what I chose to become."*
>
> —*C.G. Jung*

***

Looking for Love

Our manifestations of defense mechanisms are largely motivated by our need for acceptance and belonging. So many of us spend time talking about and thinking about love, more specifically, being in love. However, as we have previously explored, love is something that is largely intangible and when pressed on the issue, most of us cannot succinctly define what we mean by love. And, because we don't really know what love means, it is hard to know when or if you achieve what you've been searching for. If love is something that you've been seeking, take a moment of quiet reflection and ask yourself, 'How do I define love?'

When we become honest with ourselves about what we want and need, it becomes apparent that we have been using love as a catchall phrase because it is easy and feels comfortable and familiar. In reality, when we take the time to explore this (often desperate) search for love, what we may find is that we are actually seeking feelings of belonging, acceptance, physical and emotional intimacy, passion, connectedness, and safety. These desires are just a smattering of possible things we actually want to achieve by finding love, and many of us experience one or more of these on a regular basis.

However we define love, it is important to understand that not everyone gives and receives love in the same way. Of the countless ways we can show love to one another, Gary Chapman articulates five distinct ways that people can show and receive love, which appear to be relatively comprehensive and universal. These five love languages, as he calls them, are: *Words of Affirmation, Quality Time, Receiving Gifts, Acts of Service, and Physical Touch.* Let's take a moment to explore these five love languages, in no particular order of importance.

> *Words of Affirmation*: If this is your love language, unsolicited compliments mean the world to you. Hearing the words, "I love you," and hearing the reasons behind that love will be the most important to you.
>
> *Physical Touch*: A person whose primary language is Physical Touch is, not surprisingly, very touchy. Hugs, pats on the back, holding hands, and thoughtful touches on the arm, shoulder, or face is proof of the feelings shared.
>
> *Acts of Service*: These people rarely ask for help, however, anything you do to ease the burden of responsibilities weighing on an 'Acts of Service' person will speak volumes.
>
> *Quality Time*: This is not simply spending time in each other's orbit of personal space. This is defined as the person not only giving you their undivided attention, but also making time to be with you.
>
> *Receiving Gifts*: Don't mistake this love language for materialism; the receiver of gifts thrives on the love, thoughtfulness, and effort behind the gift. The gift or gesture shows that you are known, cared for, and prized above whatever was sacrificed to bring the gift to you.

In order to decipher which of these would be your primary love language, think of times when a particular action or behavior made you feel that this person cares deeply for you. This will be your primary and desired language. When you are able to identify your love language, you are then able to ask it of your significant other. Most couples that come in for counseling complain that they do not feel loved or that their love is not appreciated in the relationship.

Emotionally, people need to receive love in a way that their subconscious can accept; typically it is either in their primary or secondary love language. Keep in mind that the way an individual receives love could be very different from the way they demonstrate or express love. This nuance can make things more challenging in intimate relationships, both romantic and otherwise. Awareness, however, is key to successful 'loving' relationships.

For example, my primary love language is acts of service. Let's say I get home from a late night at the office and there are flowers waiting for me (*receiving gifts*); of course I would feel happy and appreciative. On the other hand, if on the same night I come home and the dishes have been done, the toys have all been put away and dinner is prepared, I would feel overwhelmed with love and know that my partner truly cares for me because they took the time to take this off of my hands for a night. Overall, it comes down to knowing what's important to people so you can understand, empathize, and work with them a little better. Everyone is different. We all have different life experiences; we come from different backgrounds. It makes sense that we communicate differently, too.

Breaking the Habit, Linkin Park

Memories consume like opening the wounds
I'm picking me apart again
You all assume
I'm safe here in my room
Unless I try to start again
I don't want to be the one the battles always choose
'cause inside I realize that I'm the one confused

I don't know what's worth fighting for
Or why I have to scream
I don't know why I instigate
And say what I don't mean
I don't know how I got this way
I know it's not alright
So I'm breaking the habit
I'm breaking the habit tonight

4.   Storming

Where Awareness Leads to Challenging the Self

The third step begins to really address the process of change. This is the point where we often encounter the most resistance and anxiety. Admittedly, in this phase, not only will the behaviors be examined, but they will be challenged and ultimately, if we are successful, changed. This is the most difficult phase because at this point you have achieved some level of awareness and your normal patterns of thought and behavior will start to push against the boundaries of the newer patterns you want to create and pursue.

According to the Laboratory of Neuro Imaging, the average person has about 70,000 thoughts each day! This sounds amazing and at first glance one would think that with 70,000 thoughts a day we should be happy, productive, and totally evolved. However, these are not 70,000 unique (or different) thoughts; most of these thoughts are very similar and simply repeat over and over in our heads each day, as if on a loop. Even that may not be a problem, right? Well here's the problem: the vast majority of these thoughts are negative (at best) and at times self-deprecating.

An important insight about suffering is that it comes from our thoughts. Of course, we have painful experiences, but there is a difference between experiencing pain and experiencing suffering. Pain is a physical or emotional sensation that we feel immediately, and then it passes. Suffering is the subsequent story that follows the pain. The stream of thoughts could last hours, days, months, and even years after the painful experience.

Since negative self-talk is not a natural occurrence, we have to think about the source of these thoughts. Unfortunately, many of the messages are deeply ingrained—often times stemming from early childhood, typically from parents, caregivers, or teachers. Other sources of messages are our classmates, friends, associates and the media. All of these sources project messages that we perceive as telling us we aren't good enough, pretty enough, thin enough, smart enough, or successful enough. Based on these messages, we develop an internal dialogue which ends up comprising a major portion of our 70,000 daily thoughts.

I hate those conversations that you replay in your head over and over as though on a reel. I'm thinking mostly about those conversations at work and social settings because the replay, ramifications, and meanings of conversations with intimates are much more nuanced. No matter how bad your short-term memory may be in general, in these instances, you remember e-v-e-r-y-t-h-i-n-g! Every missed opportunity to say what you wanted or needed to say. You analyze every word spoken and assign deeper meaning to it. Every glance, pause, and utterance has 1000 different interpretations, each one more insidious than the first. In these moments I have felt inadequate, because I should've handled things better.

It is the conversational analog to that deep-rooted belief that I am not good enough and the instant replay that helps me figure out whether others have realized my secret…that I am inadequate, that I feel like an imposter at almost every possible juncture. I use the conversation as a 'self-check', during my reflection I find myself internalizing the message that 'I have to do better', and 'I have to learn to camouflage my inadequacies in more intricate ways'. I am exhausted already thinking of all the work this will take. I know it is necessary because somewhere in me I believe that if they were to see the real me, I'd be fired, unfriended, or somehow lose favor in someone's eyes. What I don't know is why this matters so much to me.

Dr. Brene Brown, in her recent book *Rising Strong (2015)*, suggests that, in essence, we have to sift through the external messages we receive about ourselves to determine which ones we want to integrate into our self-definitions. While criticism with the intention to help us grow has value, most of the negative messages we have received throughout our life are not meant to move us to the next level but rather to keep us stunted where we are. When we receive these negative messages, any message really, we have three choices. First, accept it unquestioningly and let it become part of our self-definition. Second, reject it and become the person that 'doesn't care what anyone thinks'. And finally, listen critically, and then assess the message and the messenger.

"So often we find ourselves in places we don't want to be— mental strongholds that quickly begin to feel like prisons of our own making. Once we finish shaking our fists at the universe and throwing tantrums about the 'unfairness of it all' or the (often multiple) curveballs life throws us that place us securely back in these undesirable places, we have a choice to make. And really, the more I think about it, the more I realize that this is one of the only real choices we ever make in life—curl into a ball and accept the shit storms of life, or fight!

I wish I fully understood what that single motivating factor is that moved and continues to move me from 'curl up and take it' to fight, but I don't. That being said, I have done both. I have laid down and let the unhappiness of life wash over me like waves carrying me closer and closer to the edges of existence with each rising tide and I have fought. I prefer to fight.

Yesterday, I was sitting outside and there was a brief moment when the sun broke through the clouds and my new puppy wasn't being neurotic. In that moment, I felt free. That freedom has always been elusive. I realize that much of my unhappiness throughout my life has come from feeling trapped. Never physically, I've moved more than most people I know. But I've always felt trapped by expectations, both my own and those of others. In those moments when I don't feel my environment or those people around me being fully supportive, I felt like a prisoner.

In the past I have accepted it. Choosing to make myself accommodate or even assimilate to what was asked, required, or simply expected of me while suppressing my own passions and desires. But this time my choice to fight was because, for once, my own desires seemed more important. Being 'me' seemed more relevant than trying and failing at being whoever they wanted me to be.

I acknowledge that I don't fully know what it means to be 'me'. I haven't figured out yet how to integrate all of the fragmented components of my personality quite yet, but I will. I think part of being free is realizing that I am a study in contradictions and not trying to force myself to be different. I can be the quiet girl who sits in the corner with a book and the scholar with dreams of changing the world. In developing into who I want to be, I am erasing 'or' from my vocabulary. I am this AND that...and maybe a little bit of something else. I am complicated and unique and flawed and I have the freedom to accept all of that."

Those of us who have loops and loops of negative messages running through our heads at this very moment have taken option one. Don't be embarrassed if you have in the past or are currently taking this option in your life. It is the path of least resistance, although it may also be the most damaging. For those of us (yes, we fall in this camp) who at times have developed the 'I don't care' attitude, we may not have integrated the negative messages into our psyche but we do not come out unscathed, because "not caring what people think is its own hustle. The armor we have to wear to make not caring a reality is heavy, uncomfortable, and quickly obsolete" (Browne, 245). And finally, for those who assess the message and the messenger, the key is to determine whether the message is true, meaningful, or valuable, and whether the perspective or opinion of the messenger truly matters to you. When we take this critical approach and are honest with ourselves, I venture to guess that more often than not the answer to that question is a resounding no.

If you have not taken the time to critically examine and discard messages that are not useful and may be downright hurtful or harmful, this is the perfect time to do so. You have the power and ability to rewrite those messages. In much the same way that repeatedly being told that you are unworthy, burdensome, ugly, or unintelligent can result in your believing and internalizing those messages, adopting and repeating positive affirmations can become a part of your internal dialogue.

Truth: There are events in our life that become monumental. Some of these events are good. Others are bad. However the ones that affect us the most deeply come with nefarious intent and at the end of the day we find ourselves breaking. Standing at the edge of some chaos or disaster either external to us or possibly of our own making that we feel perfectly ill-equipped to deal with. Yet, here we stand. In one hand and in more than half of your heart, you hold onto the 'you' that you were before. In the other... the unknown. You know that you will never be quite the same, but at the same time, you are uncertain exactly how you will be changed. Often, the not knowing is the scary part. It feels like the ground beneath you has given way and you are falling with no idea where you will land.

You look in the mirror and feel lost, immediately recognizing the rift between who you were leading up to that moment and who you are to become in the 'after'. Eventually, the smoke clears, the chaos becomes somehow less chaotic, time elapses, putting some degree of distance between us and whatever trauma we experienced. Eventually, it feels less raw and we begin to figure things out. We are still here, but frequently our emotions are more guarded, our love less free, ourselves less whole.

An important part of this process is connecting your physical self with your neurons, psyche, and intuition; because what our bodies do, our subconscious learns from and thereby creates new pathways to be used in the future. It's not always a matter of simply telling our minds 'Don't think this or that negative thought right now'. Because, unfortunately, our minds don't listen...we do just the opposite and start to think about that negative thought. As the famed psychotherapist Carl Jung said, "What you resist persists."

When she asked me who I trusted, I answered almost instinctively. I am just as certain about the support, love and even gentle pushes in the right direction I will receive from these two as I am that the sun will rise again tomorrow. Having grown from a child who trusted no one and didn't believe in the concept of permanence or even of lasting relationships, I was at first proud of myself for learning to trust. But now, I am alone. Hours after the conversation and I have this nagging sense of unease that I can't shake. I want to ignore it.

My protector—the constant presence that keeps me from going too far down rabbit holes—is begging me to push the feeling aside. But it's too late; I've already recognized and acknowledged it. As I try to unpack what I am feeling, I realize that I am, in fact, quite comforted by having these two people in my life. It gives me peace and a quiet strength to face challenges and to be bold. The realization that is causing me angst is that neither of the two people is me.

I do not trust myself. I don't feel strong. I am all too aware of the countless times when I have made choices that benefited others and caused me physical or emotional pain. I have not always looked out for my own best interests or stood up for myself. I have been known to sabotage even my own best attempts to live a happy and fulfilled life. My reality has been that I cannot be trusted. There is no escaping this. I could ignore it if I wanted to but it wouldn't help me move beyond this. I want to understand how this lack of trust in myself has affected me. I want to end the self-limiting cycle that I know is operant in my life at this very moment whether I can recognize it or not.

Changing the Internal Dialogue

Eventually we come to a point where we are ready for change. We recognize that our patterns have hurt and hindered us and, that in order to move forward, we have to change. Gone is the time when we could comfortably ignore the issues or problems that we encounter and even the times when we could simply examine our options and desires to determine whether change is really necessary or desirable. We are right there, at the precipice of something great. It is necessary to acknowledge that sheer desire is not enough to actualize change. As much as we may try, we cannot just will ourselves into a new way of being. We need actual tangible plans that we can implement to move us towards the life that we want to live.

Because we are taught to be comfortable with the way things are and weary of change, the idea that we have the power to act and make things different may seem totally foreign. However, change requires action. For example, according to the trans-theoretical model of behavior change, action requires purposive and overt changes or modifications that reduce our risk or improve our situations. Action is observable. As you start to implement these actions into your life, you will likely begin to truly feel like you are making change.

Sometimes, the actions are subtle, like changing our self-talk. We've all heard of positive affirmations and may have even tried one or two of them ourselves in the past. The motivation for doing these are varied and when we set out with the intention to change, they become a powerful tool.

Copy the list of affirmations below. If at all possible, do this activity by hand and not using a computer; studies show that there is something very powerful about the act of writing things out that connects us to what we are writing in a way that does not typically occur when we are typing. Once you have written the list, read it daily, even if it feels a bit corny at first. As you continue your daily reading of your list, the statements will become more familiar and less awkward. By saying them out loud, you give yourself the opportunity to begin to truly hear and digest them. When you start hearing these affirmations, you start to believe and when you believe them, your awareness grows and you move closer to changing your self-talk which has the potential to catapult you into change in other areas of your life.

Don't worry if it feels uncomfortable or even unnatural at first. There are some statements that are going to be more difficult than others to even speak out loud. Pay attention to those statements because they may be your landmines—areas so packed with emotion because of past experiences that they end up being triggers.

Daily Affirmations.

1. I have a right to exist.
2. I am capable of taking full charge of my own life.
3. I have a right to ask for and expect something in life.
4. I trust myself, my feelings, and my thinking.
5. I have a right to make mistakes.
6. I have a right to be wrong.
7. I have within myself the answers to all my needs.
8. I can fill all my needs if I am willing to pay the price.
9. I am a success to the degree that I feel warm and loving towards myself.
10. I am just as worthy as anyone in the entire world.
11. I do not need to prove myself.
12. Sacrifice of myself for another is meaningless. (Note: we understand that compromise—where part of the needs of both being met—is healthy and necessary in a relationship, but sacrifice is different.)
13. I am the center of my universe, my world revolves around me. (Note: It may seem selfish, but if you are not healthy, others around you will be impacted negatively.)
14. The most important thing to my loved ones happiness is that I am happy first.
15. I am the most important, interesting person in my life.
16. The ultimate approval of myself comes from me.
17. The ultimate acceptance of myself comes from me.
18. I can decide to change my life and do it.
19. I am responsible for my life and where I am right now.
20. I am responsible for my decisions.
21. I am responsible for my own happiness.
22. I have a right to choose for myself.
23. I can dare to see what I see.

24. I can dare to think what I think.
25. I can dare to question anything.
26. I can dare to feel what I feel.
27. I have a right to come to my own conclusions.
28. I am my own authority.
29. I can dare to be me.
30. I am okay.
31. I can make things happen.
32. I can get it for myself.
33. I am a capable person.
34. I am a competent person.
35. I am an intelligent person.
36. I am a beautiful person.
37. I am perfect as I am.
38. I am a worthwhile person.
39. I will survive.
40. I can dare to take a risk.
41. I am entitled to good.
42. I decide.
43. I choose to be happy.
44. I can ask for what I want.
45. I can say what I feel.
46. I am free to be me.
47. I choose… (Identify for yourself what you want to manifest in your life: joy, passion, excitement, physical strength, financial stability and gain, secure attachment with my children, etc.)

Remember: "All that we are is the result of what we have thought. The mind is everything. What we think we become."

—Buddha

***

Emotional Triggers

My greatest hope for you is that, throughout your process of self-discovery, you will be able to transform your thinking and regain the power over your existence and your experience.

Although you may not consciously remember a time where you felt truly powerful, we are using the word 'regain' intentionally because at some point, you were in control of your existence; even if it were before, you were aware or in small ways that were almost imperceptible. This may have been a time before the world, society, your family, or *your failures* convinced you that you were not enough. But over time you will regain this power and control.

Even after awareness, growth, and confidence is reached, there will be times where you encounter an emotional trigger. In those instances, you will experience a sudden emotional reaction to an event based on the perception that a value has been violated or a need has not been met. This may well throw you off kilter and you may feel as though you are back to square one.

"I am off of autopilot. The immediate threat has passed. I made it through what, for most, would be traumatic, and barely batted an eyelash. Sure, I shed a few tears and slept a lot. I even indulged in a pint (or two) of ice cream, but I didn't feel it. You can't feel and still make it through. Feelings will break you! So, like in every other tough thing I've gone through, I put my head down and moved mechanically through tragedy like a champion.

But, like any other extreme athlete, whether participating in a triathlon or running a marathon, at some point, the race/event is over and you are just thankful to have survived it and finished. It isn't until a little time has passed and the adrenaline has begun to decrease in your system that you can truly reflect. It is in that quiet space of reflection that I was met with the full weight of my grief.

These are the messages I hear in the silence... 'My attempts to be a mother have failed'. 'I have failed'. 'Your body cannot sustain life'. 'Nothing good will ever come from you'. 'You should give up now, the next time could end poorly, too...maybe worse than before'. I want to use my coping skills to quiet the voices that are reverberating from all the walls and crevices in my head but I cannot. I feel too weak. I am consumed with this immense sense of loss. It envelops me. Its spindly arms wrap around me like a strait jacket and I am immobilized. I do not have the will to get loose.

    The voices only get louder. I want to shut them up but I can't. I believe them. That's what scares me. The voices are my own and I can't say for sure that they aren't speaking truth. Recognizing that gives me a modicum of control back; I'm still immobilized by grief; however, it has unleashed its grips from my throat and the straight jacket feels more like an uncomfortable hug than a brutal punishment. I can breathe again.

    As clarity returns slowly, I know that simply trying to quiet the voices isn't enough. I have to confront the messages and reveal the lie buried within each of them. Only when I can separate the fact from the fiction and the fear from the future will I be able to move through this grief freely...only then will I be able to heal."

Unfortunately, in life, we cannot eliminate these triggers. They are formed during childhood and throughout our lives based on a variety of life experiences that led to the five basic needs, as set forth by Maslow, either being met or not met. This is the origin of our values. If we take the time to do so, it may be possible to identify those experiences from our past that helped to shape these values and created these triggers.

When your brain perceives a threat to these values (which is what we label as a trigger), it often reacts with an emotional response, whether it be anger, denial, deflection, or another response we deem appropriate for the circumstance. Our triggers are set off when a threat is present; it is our way of attempting to protect ourselves from getting hurt yet again. Thus, we can think of them as an adaptive survival technique; you are taking action to protect yourself. Unfortunately, these self-protective attempts are often unhealthy and lead to communication or relational conflicts. The triggers will not dissipate; in fact, that is not even our goal. Instead, we should endeavor to get to a place where we can recognize our triggers, their origins, and become fully aware of how these triggers manifest behaviorally. When you arrive at that place, you are better able to evaluate and respond to life situations, instead of reacting blindly.

Only *you* can heal your triggers, so take a little time to go to a quiet place inside to reflect. Remember to be patient, kind, and compassionate with yourself because these triggers are often long-held and deeply rooted. Although delving into our triggers may be an emotional and potentially painful experience, it is necessary if we want to stop simply reacting to the world around us. As mentioned in the beginning of this journey, only when you are aware of your worldview—your perceptions and values originating from childhood experiences—and understand how it impacts your thought patterns, are you able to anticipate the feelings that will be conjured—triggers. These thoughts lead to feelings and it is the feelings that lead to behaviors. Our actions and behaviors inevitably create a consequence, which may begin the cycle again. By having this awareness of your worldview, you are able to effectively evaluate your environment and reaction to the situation. When you possess this awareness, you ultimately possess the power to choose your response.

***

How Do We Heal?

Given all that we have worked to uncover and process (or work through), there will still be times when things go awry, when we are faced with emotional suffering caused by either a need not being met, or the violation of a value, or possibly a combination of both. These violations cause emotional pain, especially when they are perpetrated by those from whom we wish to receive love. It is in these instances when we become most aware that our love language and desire for belonging, acceptance or deep regard is contradicted.

Insults can leave you shattered and are not easily forgotten (Words of Affirmation). Distractions, postponed dates, or the failure to listen can be especially hurtful (Quality Time). The absence of thoughtful everyday gestures, missed birthday, anniversary, or a hasty, thoughtless gift may be disastrous (Receiving Gifts). Laziness, broken commitments, and creating additional work communicates to receivers of this language that their feelings don't matter (Acts of Service). And finally, neglect or abuse can be unforgivable and destructive (Physical Touch). As you can see, your love language could be your greatest source of suffering when violated or ignored.

Just as Chapman's love languages help us to feel affection when it is given in the way we specifically receive, the same is true for the ways in which we receive apologies. Although, possibly less well known, there are five languages of apology. The following represent the languages of apology: Expressing Regret, Accepting Responsibility, Repentance, Requesting Forgiveness, and Making Restitution.

> ***Expressing regret***: If the person you've hurt has this language, they want to know "Do you understand how deeply your behavior has hurt me?" Communicating in this language is required for the person that has been hurt to see that you are able to empathize and put yourself in their shoes. Simply put, they want to know that you understand them as a person and you recognize how much your behavior has caused them suffering, and that you also have an understanding and recognition of the fact that they felt hurt by the behavior. In order to make amends, you must be able to pull from their values and past history and acknowledge how your behavior has triggered their values and apologize for the pain that was inflicted.
>
> ***Accepting responsibility***: If this is a person's primary apology language, they need you to take ownership for what you did or said and acknowledge that it was wrong. This person needs to hear that you are taking full responsibility for your hurtful actions without attempting to justify or diminish the impact of your behavior.
>
> ***Making restitution***: If someone has this apology language, what they really want to know is 'does this behavior reflect how you feel about me?' Harsh

or offensive words or behaviors are often interpreted as unloving, thereby triggering the dissonant question of how you could love them and still do whatever you did. In this situation, the person is looking for ways you can rebuild the trust that was lost through actions. These actions will then serve to overwrite or negate the messages that were delivered through the harmful behavior or words. Rebuilding this trust is not necessarily going to be an easy task. According to the Nobel Prize-winning scientist Daniel Kahneman, each day we experience approximately 20,000 moments. The quality of our days is determined by how our brains recognize and categorize our moments—either as positive, negative, or just neutral. Rarely do we remember neutral moments. John Gottman founded the ratio of 5:1 in that it takes five positive moments for our brains to overcome one negative moment.

Genuinely expressing the desire to change your behavior: If your apology does not include a desire to change your behavior, an individual for whom this is their primary language of apology feels that you have not truly apologized or that the apology is insincere. The person fears that if you are not expressing a desire to change that these hurtful behaviors will continue and that perhaps in a few days, weeks, or months, they will be in the same situation yet again.

Requesting forgiveness: If you offend someone who has this apology language, the words 'will you please forgive me?' are the words they want and need to hear in order to move forward. Requesting forgiveness is the way to touch their heart and is the way that feels most sincere to them. They want to see that the other person is able to be humble and offer the power to the person who was hurt.

Many of us are unaware that we even have a language of apology. For most, it is not something that we consciously think about or that we are even able to communicate to others. However, we have all had interactions when our primary language of apology has been disregarded, instances where we've been deeply hurt, and apologies or attempts to rectify the situation have fallen flat leaving us with the feelings of being misunderstood and let down. Intuitively, we want to be seen, heard, and understood. When we don't feel that those things are occurring, it may feel like 'they' just don't get you and maybe aren't even trying. The more we care, the more hurt we are when our apology language is ignored or neglected.

I am stripped of my defenses. All I think of is betrayal; this word is whispered over and over again in my ears. I am stunned and motionless. And then it all hits me at once—this agony that sears through my being. It chips away from within, and no one sees how many layers have been taken away until I am brittle inside, where even the slightest of emotions destroys any shred of composure I have left. Betrayal.

*You say that you are **sorry**.*

Can you see me? Can you see what your words meant to me? Can you see that I felt unworthy and rejected? Can you see that it tore away the years of worth I had finally been able to build up? Can you see that your words brought back that child; the delicate, yearning child who did everything they could to be loved? Can you see the dazed and confused look in my eyes that screamed that this cannot be happening to me...again?

And yet, you are sorry. You are sorry for what you said. You didn't mean it.

I trusted you. I opened my world to you. I allowed you into the darkest corners of my soul. I was bare; no masks, no delusions, and no games. I shared my strength and darkness equally. I let you inside where there are stitches from my shattered heart. I let you inside where I hold the laughter of my children. I let you inside where music gets me through what words cannot convey... I let you in and I let you see me. I let you see me in a way very few people ever get to experience. I placed my heart in your hands and you dropped it. You didn't protect me. You shared that bubble with those unworthy. You allowed strangers to look at the pieces of me that are sacred. My identity, my reality, my truth. All exposed, to be snared and ridiculed and criticized.

A life time of trauma has taught me that not everyone can be allowed inside. I've seen the horrors of which the human race is capable. I was always running, always hiding, always defending, and always surviving. Do you remember? Do you remember how I would recoil when you asked me what happened to me and who did this to me? Who made me this way? Do you remember? You said to let you teach me to love again, to feel again, and to trust again. You said you won't hurt me like they did, won't break me like they did, won't discard and dismiss me like they did.

But you did... and you are sorry. You didn't mean it.

On some nights, sadness envelops in ways that I feel myself melting away. Some nights, I need to cry some more and I'll drown if I don't. Some nights, I am swimming in unwept tears. Some nights, I feel something welling up inside of me; a wild feeling of rage and anger. Some nights, I feel nothing at all.

But. You. Are. Sorry.

An apology will only serve as healing when it is given the way we receive. As in the vignette, 'I'm sorry' was not enough to heal and repair the violation of her values. A simple proclamation of 'sorry' fails to sew the gaping wounds created by the broken trust and mishandled obligations. Here, what was needed, what the individual needed and wanted to hear, was an expression of regret and an acceptance of responsibility. 'I'm sorry' cannot begin the process of healing and forgiveness when so much more is needed.

There will be times when you are so deeply hurt that the damage is irreparable. In those instances, even apologies spoken in the language that resonates most with us may be insufficient to heal the damage and restore our relationships to their previous state. These instances are the exception, because barring severe intentionally inflicted trauma or knowing attempts to attack or destroy the things we value most, the majority of the slights we suffer can be forgiven. There are also times when we desperately need apologies that will never come, either because the person is unwilling or unable to apologize (e.g., they may have passed away before an apology could be offered). In those instances, our language of apology is irrelevant and we must learn to cope and forgive in the absence of an apology.

In the majority of cases, the things for which we require or desire apologies for are forgivable and the person from whom we need the apology is able to render it. Unfortunately, what often happens is that we find ourselves in positions where we are unable to fully accept the apology offered, typically because it is in a language that we don't interpret as being sincere. This causes confusion and frustration on the part of both individuals. The person offering the apology might be unable to understand why their attempts to apologize are inadequate for you. And, in those times, you may feel irritated or confused or despondent because people (or that particular person) just don't understand what you are feeling and what you need; while frustrating, this is not an atypical response. In those instances, if you desire to forgive and move beyond the hurt, it may be necessary to sit down and talk to the person and actually explain exactly what you need to hear and why.

As is the case with other values, our languages of love and apology can be associated with expectations that were either met or remained unmet during our childhood or earlier experiences. These values may have begun to take shape even before we were consciously aware and, again, were likely impacted by our immediate family (parents, siblings), extended family (grandparents) and other influential adults (caregivers, teachers, close family friends). To better understand the 'root' of how these values were developed, think back to a time in your childhood or early adulthood when your feelings were hurt and you needed a person you cared for deeply to 'make things right'. If this person was able to apologize and then rectify or remedy the situation, this would typically result in the development of a secure and open way of handling disappointment and accepting apologies. However, if this person was incapable of communicating in the language you received best, then your trust and ability to openly accept apologies may have been compromised, motivating your current behavior.

These past experiences contribute to how we define our language of apology today. It is because we didn't receive sincere apologies early on and often were without closure on things we felt were important that now motivates us to look for, and possibly demand, that our language of apology be respected with our significant others and other individuals with whom we are in intimate or close relationships. When you've allowed people to see you, you develop a genuine expectation and trust that they will understand you and respect your languages of both love and apology. That is why we hold them to a higher standard and require more than we would from a stranger on the street.

Take my father, for example. During my childhood, he never apologized. It didn't matter how wrong he was in the situation, he would never accept responsibility for the situation or his complicity in it or simply say 'this was wrong, it shouldn't have happened'. My father's inability to communicate responsibility and acknowledge the hurt that he caused, created in me, a need to find this in others. As an adult, I have found myself going through life demanding and holding people to what, at times, seems like an impossible standard because I don't want to subject myself to that kind of hurt and pain again.

Conversely, take a father who apologizes a million times without saying that he won't commit the same indiscretion or hurt you in the same way again. This will be detrimental for a person that needs to feel that along with the acknowledgement of wrongdoing comes a sincere desire to change—and even the subsequent actions necessary to show that change is occurring. Apologies for missed obligations and broken promises followed by more time spent sitting at the window waiting for daddy to come pick you up or come visit may create a pattern where every instance of someone not standing behind their word triggers feelings of abandonment, desperation, and unworthiness. Apologies without action or repeated instances of disappointment may cause irreparable damage to a relationship with this individual.

Thus, as you can see, it is important to know who you are dealing with and what they need to hear. It is also important that we are sensitive to the ways in which these triggers develop and are gentle with ourselves and others when we feel that a particular response may be an overreaction to a given circumstance.

"Study me as much as you like, you will never know me. For I differ a hundred ways from what you see me to be. Put yourself behind my eyes, and see me as I see myself. Because I have chosen to dwell in a place you can't see."

—Rumi

***

Communication

Communication is essential to all successful relationships. Be it with family, friends, romantic partners, or colleagues, communication helps us to arrive at shared understandings, allowing us to more easily resolve differences of opinion and conflict that may be encountered. In theory, it should be a simple, almost intuitive process. We, as humans, are social creatures. We learn to communicate, both verbally and non-verbally, shortly after entering the world, and that process continues as we grow and mature. Unfortunately, due to differences in interpretation, listening style, delivery style, and non-shared meanings, much of what we say—or mean to say—gets lost in translation, even despite our best intentions. We say one thing and our communication partner hears something else. Or, we intend for a certain message to be communicated and something completely different is inferred. Add in the difficulties inherent with communications over the various mediums available to us (i.e., email, text, and social media) and the misunderstandings can quickly escalate. These are all potential sources of conflict in communication.

It is attractive to blame our communication partner when things go awry. This isn't because we inherently want to 'pass the buck', rather it is because outside of our professional endeavors, we typically communicate from a place of emotion rather than tactic or strategy and it therefore may be difficult to identify your own responsibility when communication efforts are ineffective. When our interactions are with loved ones or close friends, we feel that they should just 'get it' and when they don't, we assign blame (i.e., they never listen) often leading to feelings of frustration and resentment. Just like with languages of love and apology, communication requires us to think about our communication partners' style and avoid unintentionally causing them to feel attacked or defensive. In short, in order to be effective, we must approach conversations (particularly those that are important or those with people you consider important or valuable) with specific skills and strategies that help to foster open communication.

We recognize the nuances that can exist given the vast array of interactions in which good communication is integral; however, there are some universal points that we must consider to avoid common traps and pitfalls. First, and possibly most importantly, we do not have the right to define anyone else's existence or perception for them. Stop and take a moment to let that sink in. Just as you are entitled to your position, your worldview, your way of being, so are they. Although many of us are taught to believe in the existence of objective truths and 'right versus wrong', the reality is that there is rarely one stance or perception that is more correct than the other. And, until one can accept this notion to be the truth, they will be incapable of having genuine or effective communication. Because, when you hold the belief that you are right and 'they' are wrong, then during a friendly debate or in the aftermath of a heated argument, you will have your guard up which will emanate through your posture, tone, and even the efficacy of your listening skills.

You will not be able to see the other person's point of view as valid, and any empathy that you are able to muster will likely be inauthentic. In these instances, you are likely to spend most of your energy drumming up a fabulous retort or sharpening your powers of persuasion, instead of hearing what is being said. So what do we recommend instead? *Listen.* Truly listen as though you really want to know what this person is thinking and try to follow their thought patterns. Try to understand their worldview.

Listen for how they came to this realization and what factors from their past experiences helped shape their ideas and values. Give them the respect and space to articulate their rationale and allow them to feel accepted as they are. Remember, intelligence allows us the ability to understand and entertain a point of view without needing to accept it.

The second essential communication principle is that in order for a person to understand where you are coming from, it is necessary to share your perceptions or viewpoint in a way that reaches past their conscious defenses. This may not be as crucial in casual conversations, but is imperative in meaningful communication. Often, instead of being transparent and vulnerable, we begin conversations by taking a defensive posture and justifying our position. We enter into the interaction already prepared to defend ourselves and the reasons why we have the right to say, feel, or think a certain way. We do this in our misguided attempt to justify our own existence, failing to remember that we already have the right to be there and be, say, and do exactly what we want! Although we may assume that we are actually advancing our position by being defensive and ready to pounce on anyone with differing viewpoints, we are not helping our communication partner to understand where we are coming from (our motivations) or to see the true passion behind our convictions.

Since meaningful communication is enhanced when the two (or more) parties are able to understand one another, our goal is often to have the other person step into our shoes and see the world the way we see it, even if only for a moment. One way to achieve this is by progressing systematically through a process to help your communication partner(s) better understand you. Adapted from Gottman (2002), the following five steps aid in allowing your partner to gain insight into your feelings and motivations:

1. State your feelings;
2. Give the reasons that explain **why** you had each one of those feelings;
3. List the triggers;

4. Assume responsibility for the role you played in the situation;
5. Identify solutions for the future.

One of the most important tools for building a healthy relationship is knowing how to process and present your position in a way that helps both partners learn from it and arrive at some sort of resolution. Step 4 is particularly useful for communication because it helps to lower the natural defensiveness of your communication partner by acknowledging that the conversation is not originating from a place of blame and that, instead, you are acknowledging your role and committing to (step 5) working together to arrive at a solution.

Months had passed since we started fighting. It seemed like every conversation that lasted more than a couple of minutes turned quickly to shame and blame in one form or another. I was guilty of it, too, although I rationalized my behavior that ranged from passive aggressive to just plain aggressive. He provokes me. He infuriates me. He is mean to me. One night as the tears flowed, I decided I wanted a different narrative. This person was a part of my life and would continue in this capacity until our dying breath. We were linked. I had to do better; we had to do better. I took out a piece of plain unlined paper and started writing...Step one.

You make me feel like you don't trust me or respect me (feeling). When you ask me questions and then hyperfocus on one thing I said or refuse to accept my answer or explanation (cause), I feel invalidated and voiceless, like what I have to say doesn't matter (trigger). I know that sometimes I try to communicate important topics when I am overly upset, and because of that, it may be difficult for you to see that what you perceive as defensiveness is just me being passionate (responsibility). As we move through this life, I will try to take a break before I approach important topics so that I can do so without getting so upset (solution).

The list continued...paragraph after paragraph. Complete with bullet points and subpoints I carefully outlined the ways in which our attempts at communication had failed. It was easier than I thought, but then again I do love making lists.

As you gain experience communicating in this manner, it will become second nature. You will find that the process facilitates easier dialogue because it is clear and provides concrete examples—important because, as you may recall, most people are better able to deal with or understand things that are tangible. Recognizing our own responsibility and being able to accept it is also huge; this avoids creating a 'you wronged me and I am totally blameless' dynamic which automatically puts people on the defense. Your responsibility might be very small, depending on the circumstances, or it might be massive; simply acknowledge it and move on. Don't get trapped in the cycle of blaming yourself for the current situation; instead, allow it to be a catalyst for change. You may feel particularly motivated if you think that a change in your behavior and/or reactions could have had a different and more desirable result. Also, the process of having identified solutions and presenting them back to your communication partner says 'I want us to figure out a way to make this better'. That small seed of hope is monumental in relationships.

"I go back and forth battling between my head and my heart. There's so much to say...

I am scared. I am frightened by the certainty of what I want. I am terrified that this arrogance will leave me broken and lost. Yesterday was both unbelievably amazing and at the same time, desperately disheartening. I was floating, wrapped in this bubble of love and joy. And then that bubble burst and I was flailing to regain sure footing. I know that we could have such a simple existence and it would be so wonderful. We have such an easy way of being and conversing. But life is not so easily compartmentalized anymore. I see the harm I am causing. I feel I am losing myself. Losing myself in a fantasy of love and romance and passion. I am risking everything I hold priceless for a love and a dream of a reality that may never come to pass. You lead your life and I have mine. You can't give yours up and neither can I. Yet, I am caught in the vortex of your being, intoxicatingly blinded by your charm. From what I have seen, you are everything I've waited for.

Right now I am overwhelmed and at times spiraling in my fears. I don't want to lose myself in those fears and I don't want to lose you either. I've studied and seen what this type of guilt can do to a relationship and I couldn't bear it if one day your love turned bitter, into resentment, because of the troubles this has brought in your life. I am also afraid of the stigma—not from society; rather I am afraid of the scorn that awaits me from your family based on my situation. For me, it's both terrifying and infuriating at the same time. The unfairness and the judgment cause the fury while the fear is from that inevitable rejection from those you hold so dear.

I have always searched for a loving and accepting family and given that it wasn't always available from my parents. I had hoped that one day I would find it from my spouses' family, but I didn't have it there either and it seems ever elusive. I posted this last year...It seems so eerie...'One day I'll wake up on a Sunday with the love of my life and make coffee and toast, and all will be alright.' Well, I have found that person. I've wanted someone who was kind and funny and intelligent and accepting and protective and one who will challenge me to grow as a person, someone who has an open mind who could look outside the box and accept it even if you don't agree. Someone who would adore me and make an effort to show that affection through their thoughtfulness, time, and acts of service. Someone who enjoys classic style as much as I do; someone with the same desire to explore different cultures and the beauty this world has to offer. Someone with a curious mind to keep me on my toes. Someone with a sense of rhythm and love for music. I've always wanted someone who would sing to me. Someone who values respect and will take measures, at necessary times, to make sure that is delivered. Someone who would fight for me.

A person that could truly understand is the rarity of my love. Someone to treasure the pieces of me others view as broken. Someone who is independent and has a secure sense of who they are and are constantly learning and growing to understand themselves. Someone who is willing to appreciate how I see the world. Someone who is proud of what I have to offer; who is not threatened by my magnificence. Someone who will honor my sense of freedom and individuality and allow me to be free. Someone who feels that as long as they have me, nothing else matters and there will be that security and certainty that my emotional needs would be met.

In the short time I've been re-acquainted with you, you have shown me all of these things in one way or another. It's daunting; I so desperately want to trust it. I am afraid of what will happen to me if I do."

Being able to invoke this communication style is especially beneficial in conflict resolution. It is often difficult for people to experience true empathy in high emotion situations, especially in those situations where you feel compelled to protect and promote your own position. However important, empathy is not instinctual for everyone and may be situational (e.g., I can empathize under the following conditions). Since not everyone can empathize effectively, we believe that being able to see the validity of a contrasting point or worldview, whether we fully accept or adopt it, can help move communication forward instead of bringing it to a screeching halt.

> In the aftermath of a fight or regrettable incident, you can use the following format to increase understanding between you and your partner. It is crucial for you to understand that in any given argument, there is no absolute 'reality' as to what happened. There are always two 'subjective realities' or perspectives. It is never a matter of who is right and who is wrong, but how the two of you can come to understand each other, accept responsibility, and find your points of compromise so that you can move forward together.
>
> —*Ellie Lisitsa*

Brand New Sun, Jason Lytle

Here,
Grab a broken branch
With a sunburnt hand
In a washed up land

Soon,
We should rest a while
We're like a tired child
It's been a lot of miles.

I might fall down
And my back is bad
We might fall down
On a sleeping back.

So you should hold my hand
While everything blows away

And we'll run,
To a brand new sun.
We will run,
To a brand new sun.

Damn,
How did it get so bad?
With all the dreams we had
Now you seem so sad.

You should hold my hand
While everything blows away
And we'll run
To a brand new sun.

5. Working

Putting Theory to Practice

The Fourth Phase is where you will take everything you have discovered thus far throughout your transformative process and put those things into practice. At this point, you have already determined that you are no longer satisfied with or willing to accept the status quo and you have taken steps to identify the root causes and motivations for your values, beliefs, and behaviors. You have moved beyond simply wanting to change and you are ready to change and begin to manifest the life you envision. Although there is still much work to do, and there will be bumps along the way, much of the emotional hard lifting is done.

Before moving forward you should take stock of the ways that you have grown and changed and the progress made thus far. Although it may at first feel self-congratulatory, you should celebrate all growth in the right direction and be proud of your newfound motivation and enhanced self-insight. Be explicit in identifying the growth and change and avoid the common trap of taking these things for granted. They are not inevitable; it is absolutely possible to grow older but not wiser. However, you worked hard to get where you are and, in doing so, you are embracing your potential to live your best life. Whereas you may have lived hours, days or decades without self-awareness, you likely have now arrived (or will soon arrive) at a place where you can recognize and articulate the magnificence of who you are.

"I am"

"I am intuitive; I am watchful. I can feel emotions of those around me and feel it into the depths of my bones. I am the

giggles of my children—the warmth in their arms. I am the fiery breath of a dragon; intimidating and fierce. I am the teardrops of my friends. My soul is fire and wine, I am never cold blooded; I am incapable of doing anything without feeling, never indifferent. I speak from deep within my strata and boil over as fast as a pan of water on the stove. I am the priestess of the moon—powerful and alluring those who are broken. I am in the gaze; the powerful piercing, paralyzing gaze of a cougar. I am the excitement before the summer storm. I am the challenging rise of the eyebrow. I am the breath, and heartbeat of my sun and moon. I am the spirit and knowledge—a constant pursuit of growth and acceptance. I am the love—silent, searching and finding, and forever unbroken. I am the scars of the past— wounded, healed, reinjured and sewn back. I am the sway of the hips, shimmy of the shoulders moving to the shimmering ribbons of music—of art. I am Zahir*, in Arabic meaning possessing the power to be unforgettable."

—Zahir: conceptualized by Paulo Coelho

When you are ready, challenge yourself to complete the statement 'I am…' This should be more than just a sentence— although that is a tremendous beginning. Dig deep and be as abstract as you need to be. Think of what makes you uniquely, undeniably you. Think of how you see yourself existing and moving through this world. Again, we recognize that even after all of the growth you have accomplished, this process can be hard. We know this because we have struggled with accomplishing this task also. Do not be discouraged. When you have spent a lifetime—or even fragments of a lifetime—being made to believe that you are inadequate or unworthy, it is difficult to imagine yourself as anything more. The task becomes incrementally more difficult when we experience additional negative events, betrayal, and rejections that reaffirm our deeply held beliefs in our own inadequacies.

While we hope you are on a high of self-discovery as you engage in this process so that completing the 'I am' activity is an articulation and reaffirmation of your existence, we understand that not everyone has reached that point. Even if you are in one of the darker moments and find yourself questioning your worth, the 'I am' activity is a useful tool to help gather strength and shape your reality. Our brains are capable of transforming anything when given the opportunity to do so. It isn't magic (unfortunately) and it won't happen immediately, but by creating an image of who we are or who we want to be, we can start to build new neuropathways in our brains that will override the old messages and reflect our new beliefs.

***

Power Image

Although ideal, this is a scary proposition for some. We become so caught in our negative cycles that the hope for something greater seems too big to grasp. Sometimes we avoid growth because we are comfortable and the unknown, with all its excitement and possibility, exists far beyond our comfort zones.

"Our deepest fear is not that we are inadequate.
Our deepest fear is that we are powerful beyond
Measure.
It is our light, not our darkness that most frightens
Us.
We ask ourselves; Who am I to be brilliant, gorgeous,
talented, fabulous?
Actually, who are you not to be?
Your playing small does not serve the world.
There is nothing enlightened about shrinking so that
other people won't feel insecure around you.
We are all meant to shine, as children do.
We were born to make manifest the glory of God that is
within us.
It's not just in some of us; it's in everyone.
And as we let our own light shine, we unconsciously
give other people permission to do the same.
As we are liberated from our own fear, our presence
automatically liberates others."

(Marianne Williamson, 1992—often attributed to
—Nelson Mandela)

The idea that creating an image of what we want can help establish new pathways to move us towards that desired reality is not a recent phenomenon. Throughout history, in all cultures, we find guided imagery used in healing; most commonly in Chinese, Indian and Native American traditions. Being able to create and invoke these powerful images allows you to pull out things hidden in the recesses of your mind—ideals that may be inaccessible because of years of pain and trauma.

If we examine how this works, we see that this is not an example of simply thinking yourself happy. There is a scientific basis for why this process can have beneficial effects. Specifically, connections exist between the visual and creative sphere of your brain and the involuntary nervous system. When your brain's visual cortex is activated through your mind's eye (more commonly referred to as the imagination), your involuntary nervous system is stimulated, triggering both physical and emotional responses, such as the fight-or-flight response.

The decision to fight or flee when faced with danger or other stressors may seem incomprehensible or random, and to some degree it is dictated by a very unique set of contextual circumstances surrounding a given event. However, some of what might seem instinctual or intuitive about this response to danger and stress comes from the mental images we possess and reinforce about ourselves. Numerous clinical observations suggest that an individual visualizing an imagined scene reacts both emotionally and physically as though it were actually occurring in real time (e.g., Schorr, 1974). Mental rehearsing of this type helps to remove some of the randomness from our responses and may even be able to assuage some anxiety or fear about how we will respond in a given situation.

Mental images, formed long before we learn to understand and use words, lie at the core of who we think we are. What we believe the world is like, what we feel we deserve, what we think will happen to us, and how motivated we are to take care of ourselves, are all motivated by these existing mental images. These images even influence our beliefs and attitudes about how we fall ill and what will help us to get better. While we recognize the early foundations of these mental images, we also recognize that we have tremendous power in influencing these images if we want them to be different. Learning to fully maximize the creative sphere of your brain allows for the potential and power to begin manipulating those powerful messages that lie, largely dormant and unchallenged, in your subconscious. Many ancient healing rituals involve manipulation of these images. As such, guided imagery can be considered one of the oldest forms of medicine or therapy.

Beyond the physiological response, guided imagery can work by replacing a less than positive mental image of yourself with a more positive totem or symbol of who you are or have the potential to become. The ability to call upon this totem, consciously or unconsciously, increases the likelihood that old messages of not being good enough or worthy enough will be interrupted. Counteracting the negative images establishes the most basic starting point of allowing for the emergence of the symbolic being you strive to become. Note that we didn't say that the process of implanting totems would create this new person. We intentionally avoided using this terminology because we believe strongly that the process is not about creating a new person. Instead, we believe that this strong, competent life force already exists within you. That person is already there, the power image simply gives us something tangible to connect with and invoke as we manifest this existence.

Having these invokable images assist us in effectively responding to, and not just reacting to, situations. In our common dialect, people use the words 'react' and 'respond' interchangeably, thinking that the two are actually synonymous; however, we disagree. Although similar, for practical purposes, the difference is distinct and meaningful. Say, for example, I am sitting in front of you and I throw my pen at your head without provocation. Aside from thinking I have completely lost my mind, what would you do? Would you sit and say, "I see this pen coming at me, perhaps I should reconsider my position…" or would you immediately dodge to avoid being impaled? I should hope the latter. The first option is responding while the second is reacting. Both serve a purpose in life. There are times when a split second, almost instinctual reaction may save us, yet there are other times when we would benefit more from greater introspect and a proactive approach. Unfortunately, many of us have been conditioned to react to situations that actually require a response. Along with the other skills and strategies you have learned (and hopefully mastered) thus far, power images can be called upon quickly in that small window of opportunity we have to determine whether to react or respond to a situation that would normally cause us distress.

The creation and adoption of a power image is a dynamic and fluid process. The power image we create will change based largely on our growth as individuals. Sometimes, our power image changes and shifts in ways that communicate our transitions even when we may not yet be fully conscious of these shifts. During those instances where our images shift to accommodate our growth and transitions, we can experience some fear and apprehension; especially true if we've become accustomed to our existing power image and we aren't consciously choosing for it to change. Along with whatever other transitions and traumas we might be experiencing, we can attempt to call upon our power image only to be met with something unfamiliar.

I recently went through a series of major life transitions in close succession. As I evolved and emerged from these transitions, my power image shifted from a cougar to an owl. It was in the interim between the two power images, in the very midst of my darkest moment, that I experienced the uncertainty of being faced with an image I did not consciously adopt. Over and over again during this process, when I attempted to conjure up the cougar, an image of a cobra imposed itself into my awareness. Here is where this experience becomes interesting; I have a phobia of snakes. Not a healthy aversion or fear, but a full on phobia fueled by past traumatic encounters with snakes. So, I find myself grasping for straws, trying to find strength when the entire fabric of my world is unraveling and my mind can only conjure images of my greatest fear!

I distinctly remember attempting to conjure the cougar at least two to three times in different contexts and each time I was met with the same result. A damn cobra! I was fed up with everything and everyone and I felt powerless. I found myself painfully close to turning that anger inward. But, before I did, I took a deep breath and sat down in a quiet moment of introspection to figure out what my psyche was trying to communicate. It took a moment, but I was quiet. It occurred to me that once I stripped away my initial repulsion and separated myself from my past trauma surrounding snakes, the cobra is a truly beautiful creature and the most majestic of all the snakes. The patterns, the shape, the venom, and the way it dances and moves. It weaves its spell around people and they become hypnotized at the allure. When it is least expected… it strikes. You don't hear it or see it typically until it's too late. I started to embrace it more.

Up until this point, my image—the cougar—was powerful, aggressive, pursuing, and strong. All of these characteristics made sense because that image emerged at a time in my life when I felt cornered and unable to respond in a way that was the norm for me. Before, when faced with adversity, I would fight back and assert my power and dominance and competence in the situation. Here, in attempting to better understand, I had to sit still, stay quiet, and wait. Based on past trauma, I had associated being still and quiet with failure and acquiescence. However, during that time of quiet reflection, I realized that I am still powerful. It occurred to me that at this particular time, it might not benefit me to be fierce or on the offense, but even in sitting in wait, my power was not negated. As a cobra, I can strike when provoked.

"My power image has shifted and evolved as I have throughout the years. I remember always being drawn to the wolf. Ferocious and wild. Beautiful, graceful and always surrounded by her pack. Strong on her own, but stronger with the help of her family. I was much younger at this time and I didn't have faith in my own strength. The wolf generally represents intuition, instinct, appetite for freedom, and social connection. It also represents a fear of being threatened and a lack of trust. That would make sense while being new to town

(yet again) to the third high school and having been betrayed by those who were supposed to, forever, love and protect me. Throughout the final years of high school, I experienced trauma and abuse in a way I never thought I would. I was in denial when it first happened. This cannot be my story, not like this. I didn't do anything to deserve what the universe is handing to me, throwing at me. How could so much wrong happen to one person in such a short amount of time? I can't be defined by this, by what he did to me...

As I desperately attempted to rewrite the meaning of this horrific chapter, my life continued. I graduated. I was accepted to college and I was continuing on with what seemed, from the outside, to be a successful life. No one knew what had happened. No one asked. No one recognized the light going out from behind my eyes. No one noticed the sadness behind my smile. No matter how hard I tried to continue with my life, he was still there. Still controlling, still mocking, still threatening. My father once asked what had happened to me, what made me into a shell without a soul. The trauma ensued. I had no escape. There was no escape. The shame, the blame, the stigma, the shunning from my home, from my community, the pity... I couldn't face that. I lost faith in my pack. They weren't there and at times they were also the source of my pain. That's when the cougar emerged.

The cougar represents coming into your own power and taking charge. The cougar knows how to set her boundaries and let those who cross them know that they have. She can be seen or not seen as she masters her camouflage. She embodies personal strength and elegance. I had spent the last 14 years embodying what the cougar represents. And then, I feared that slowly I had lost her. I lost my grip on my source of strength. I began to question who I am. All that I had worked to overcome, was creeping back into my daily existence... he was back. I saw him in the actions of another. As they say, the person you would take a bullet for, is at times the one pulling the trigger. I had created this beautiful life with a stranger. And as the mask fell off, so began the unraveling of my beautiful tapestry. The cobra manifested during the last months of this new version of despair.

And now, having once again fought through another chapter, I have emerged with the spirit of the owl.

The owl is emblematic of a deep connection with wisdom and intuitive knowledge. If you have the owl as totem or power animal, you're likely to have the ability to see what's usually hidden to most. When the spirit of this animal guides you, you can see the true reality, beyond illusion and deceit. The owl also offers for those who have it a personal totem the inspiration and guidance necessary to deeply explore the unknown and the magic of life."

When I finally recognized that my shifting power image was not based on weakness or failure, but on adaptation and growth, I was able to again draw strength and peace from my image. The anxiety receded leaving in its wake a calm emanating feeling of authority and strength.

The process of determining your power image or spirit animal is a personal one. You may have always known that you have an animal, a particular scenery, an object or ideal to which you are drawn. We particularly like to work with animals in this form of guided imagery because there is more depth than with an object or other source of nature. So, indulge us. When you have a few quiet moments, get comfortable, close your eyes, take several deep breaths and then try to imagine an animal, your spirit animal. What is the first animal that comes to mind? Although it might seem a bit strange at first, spend just a few seconds examining the animal. Is it large or small? Are there other characteristics? And then examine yourself, what do you feel?

When you are done, open your eyes. Now, ask yourself the following questions to gain a deeper understanding of your connection to this animal.

- What characteristics drew you to the animal you chose?
- Are there connections between your spirit animal and situations or events in your life?
- What qualities do you personally associate with your spirit animal?

- Which characteristics do you covet and wish you possessed?
- How is the animal typically portrayed by society or spiritual traditions?

Gaining a better understanding of our power images helps us to identify personal goals, particularly those surrounding how we want to behave or be viewed during tumultuous times. The process of visualizing and attempting to consciously settle on or discover your image along with the questions above will help you better understand your image and your power. During times of depression or severe anxiety, an image of a hummingbird, while not strong or ferocious, may represent the ability to remain in constant flight unfazed by life circumstances. For someone who feels like they can physically and emotionally be knocked over by the next thing that comes their way, large or small, seeing themselves as graceful and able to rise above the bullshit and just exist peacefully yet still in motion may make the difference between giving up and choosing to move through a difficult situation. This is just another in our cadre of strategies to continue to propel us towards self-actualization and learning to fully embrace yourself and your distinct path.

***

Life by Design

We make plans every day; sometimes we make to-do lists at work, shopping lists for groceries, or schedules for how we spend our day. Often we find that writing them down helps us to keep track of our goals, measure progress, and stay on target. There will be times when we feel like we are barely staying afloat while attempting to juggle these multiple, often competing demands, but, in general, we've gotten pretty good at making things work. We have learned to be successful managing the daily tasks necessary for work or school and to keep our households running. Unfortunately, we frequently forget that these same principles can apply to personal goals and overall desires for our lives as well.

Think about what you want to accomplish or goals that you want to reach. Unlike with lists of tasks or items needed from the supermarket, when thinking about your overall life goals, you don't have to be limited by the constraints of what is available or seems likely or practical; instead, dream big. Seriously, for just 10 minutes don't take reality into consideration at all; just write down exactly what it is that your heart desires—be comprehensive; leave nothing out. As you brainstorm, realism is not a criterion. When you think about your life, future, or possibilities, start with your passions. What excites you? What is worth changing or sacrificing for? Use these questions to create a description of the ideal life that you can have and all the things that you want to fit into that life. Do this in whatever format resonates most with you—list, vignette, vision board. What is important is that you begin to recognize and visualize your desires.

When I was pregnant, my driving force was fear. I was constantly scared that I wouldn't be 'enough'. These thoughts and concerns kept running through my mind on a constant loop. 'You have to be worthy of the life that you're carrying. You have to be good enough. You have to accomplish…'

This fear is what drove me to accomplish my goals and achieve my dreams. My driving force, my passion, the thing that I felt was worth sacrificing for was my babies. If I died tomorrow, I wouldn't want one more hour to clean my house or tidy the yard or exercise. I wouldn't care that the laundry was left undone. I would want one more hour snuggling on the couch with my kids, inhaling their sweetness and joy. I would want them to be certain of one thing if nothing else, that they were my reason for breathing. Although my passion is clear to me now, it wasn't always so easy to identify… My parents gave me the best they were capable of and even with that, I experienced more forms of abuse than a child should. That's why I desperately needed things to be different. I needed my children to have an existence that instilled in them the belief that they were worthy of living.

Because I hold a worldview that failure and fear are constantly lurking, I made sure to create a reality for my children that would produce in them a different outcome, instead of simply succumbing to a 'woe is me' approach to life.

Once you have identified your passion and driving force, you are ready to begin your list. Start by writing down your goals, define what they mean, and try to be as detailed as possible. Your list may include things like success, a social life, happiness, managing the anxiety associated with travel, secure attachment with children, or being in a romantic relationship. Whatever you include should be based on the life you want, just remember to be explicit. If you write down that you want to be healthy, decide on a weight range, or dress size, active lifestyle, and healthy eating. Or if you want to be successful, what does that mean? A specific salary, office space, total amount of personnel?

Success! For me, I will know I am successful when the thing I do for work also brings me joy. I will finally be able to utilize all of my talents and diverse training in a manner that will help make communities healthier (e.g., by helping them determine how to effectively lower their risk of disease, violence, or poverty). Financially, I will be compensated in a manner that I feel is consistent with my training... I see 6 figures in my future... high six figures. But more important than the money, I want a life without struggle. Being able to pay my bills and have money left over for the things I want to do and not just the things I need. For me, success means freedom and autonomy.

Once you have dreamt big and determined exactly what achievement of those dreams will look like, you can begin the process of working towards them. Now is the time that reality and practicality begin to return to the picture. We begin by breaking each of your desires and goals into more manageable tasks. In the professional world we often talk about making your goals and objectives S.M.A.R.T.: Specific, Measurable, Achievable, Relevant, and Time-Bound. Although we won't be quite this systematic in approaching your personal goals and

101

objectives, breaking them down will help you stay on track. Take each item on the list (e.g., success) and break it down into steps that you can take in the short, medium, and long term tasks. What can be accomplished today? In a month? A year? Five years? A lifetime?

For each given month per goal, break it down to something you can tackle within 24 hours, another aspect in a week, and what needs to be done within the following three weeks, all the way until the end of that month. Take writing this book. We needed to break it down to strategies and then priorities. I (Habiba) was mostly in charge of that since Shalon will readily admit that she struggles (a lot) with procrastination. I set a timeline that brought this book to fruition. When we birthed the idea I decided that, for my part, within 24 hours I needed to come up with a list of topics we intended to share with you. Within the next week, I wanted to turn that list of topics into an organized outline that more fully flushed out each desired section. Within the next month–three months, I needed to break those down first into objectives and then into subsections. Next, together we needed to write and then read all the sections, integrate our notes and narratives and then edit, edit, edit.

Steps like those described above need to be decided for each of the dreams on your list. You can work through them simultaneously or start with one or two of these dreams that you feel could be transformative to your life. Once you have accomplished one or more of these dreams that you feel are transformative, then you may begin to experience shifts in your outlook that will make accomplishing the other dreams easier. Don't get us wrong; your plan may change and your timeline may have to shift, but having one gives you a good starting place and allows you to measure your progress.

Although realism is not a factor when you are listing your dreams initially, the strategies you identify to accomplish these dreams need to be realistic in order to be effective. Be gentle with yourself. Believe that you can achieve them and you will find a way to meet them 24hrs at a time (or one hour at a time if a full day seems too overwhelming at this point).

Giving yourself deadlines is a great strategy, but also incorporating methods of accountability may help tremendously. Share your goals and proposed timeline with someone you can trust. If, at first, you have difficulty identifying a person that you are comfortable sharing with or the dreams seem too sensitive or personal to share, then journaling may be a good option to help you get started. Consider joining together with friends, family members, or even an online community with similar goals to hold one another accountable since accountability is a huge asset when you are trying to accomplish these dreams.

When I went away to college, I was 230 pounds. I was self-conscious and awkward. I had always been on the chubby side, but this was an all-time high for me. The people I encountered were new and didn't know that I was funny and sarcastic and smart. To them I was just the fat girl. I wanted to be invisible and for the most part, socially, I was. Shortly after Christmas my junior year, I went to pick up pictures from the photo counter (this was long before selfies and digital cameras). As I sat flipping through the pictures, I came across the one I had taken when my mom and brother were heading back home from a holiday visit.

I WAS HUGE. Not just chubby or overweight. I literally looked like I was wearing a fat suit. I hated what I saw and remember crying because for the first time I felt like I was getting a true glimpse of how others saw me. Instantly I could envision a physical existence that looked different. And along with that new physical being, I saw an emotional and social being that was more fulfilled, more comfortable, more confident. I wanted to be HER. But I had no idea where to start.

That very same week, I started a group-based weight loss program. I didn't know if it would work; in fact I was skeptical because I had tried other similar programs in the past and had failed miserably at all of them. But this one was different. I knew I had over 80 pounds to lose but I didn't focus on that. I made manageable goals. First, let's get to 5 pounds. Then 10. Then let's shoot for 10% of my body weight and so on and so forth, until I reached my goal. I made proclamations of goals to my group and to my friends and loved ones. I hung pictures. I talked about it openly with people.

By the time I started graduate school a year and a half later, I was 138lbs. Yes, there was some will power that was associated with the weight loss and I can't attribute it all to making small milestone tasks to accomplish and being held accountable, but I know that it helped. Having support, having people that I knew and even some that I didn't, celebrate my accomplishments with me, set me up for success. I also learned how to apply the same goal setting skills to other tasks like finishing my degrees, buying my first home, and having a baby.

Most of the goals that we have talked about up to this point have been those for which you would be solely or primarily responsible for accomplishing. The art of establishing tasks and deadlines to achieve shared goals (e.g., starting a business or deciding to partner or have a family), is a bit more nuanced. It requires trust, patience and honest, respectful introspection.

Lewis Carroll, in his classic book *Alice and Wonderland*, observed: *if you don't know where you're going, any road will get you there.* This may be an astute assessment of life and may even provide us useful advice on road trips with undetermined destinations. However, the journey to self-discovery—as we have previously pointed out—requires a purposive and thoughtful action on your part. You may not know exactly what the manifestation of your ideal self will look or feel like, but in order to get there you must take conscious efforts to arrive. Now, that being said, once you know who and what you want to become, prepare for lots of unexpected adventures along the way! It's amazing what challenges and joys life will throw at us as we grow.

With your ideal self in mind, you should now be well on your path of self-discovery. Not only do you have a vision of your ideal self and desired life goals, you have already begun the admittedly difficult process of uncovering who you are and the reasons and motivations behind that manifestation. You are now ready to focus on how to orchestrate the rest of your narrative. As you may have guessed, this process will involve unearthing and exploring messages deeply imprinted from your childhood, the values that resulted from these messages, the way these experiences have shaped your thoughts and behaviors, and the passions you want to put into practice. Carl Jung has said, "Your vision will become clear only when you can look into your own heart. Who looks outside dreams; who looks inside, awakes". This is a period of awakening.

We do not believe this to be a magical process, nor do we assume it to be particularly easy. Bringing your dreams, passions and inner visions to fruition is going to take work. What we do believe to be true, however, is that even for those putting in the work, if you don't truly believe in the real possibilities of what you want, the process will be difficult and will oftentimes result in major setbacks and roadblocks, even failure to achieve your envisioned life. That being said, as corny as it may feel sometimes, we take this visionary process very seriously. Because, in the words of Napoleon Hill, whatever the mind can conceive and believe, it can achieve.

I am a daydreamer. I always have been. I can forego television and movies and even books and instead spend moments that quickly turn to hours lost in my own imagination. I spend time crafting alternate realities where people hadn't died and things had not been lost. In those realities, I am happy...safe. Now that I'm expecting my first child, the energy I typically spend daydreaming has merged with my meditations, prayers and all the cosmic energy I can harness to create a healthy, happy tiny human, free from my emotional baggage and able to conquer the world. I want for them to be happy and to find that happiness in whatever form they choose.

So, when you look within, what do you see? Even if just for a moment, allow yourself the innocent luxury of daydreaming. Recall (or revisit) the list of values you developed earlier and also the goals you worked on to categorize your life into different aspects (e.g., social or romantic relationships, family, finances, sex, mental/spiritual health, career, body image, home, etc.) From there begin to visualize what you want.

"Change…So much change and at times I am floating, flying and falling free while other days I feel broken and completely alone. This tearing apart of what was once my norm will make way for me to piece back the puzzle that makes up my existence in order to reflect for what I have always longed. This was to be my chance to create and manifest the life I deserve; one that mirrors the person I am on the inside, important because I know that to some I am an enigma. A quote that's dear to me by Rumi states: 'Study me as much as you like, you will never know me. For I differ a hundred ways from what you see me to be. Put yourself behind my eyes, and see me as I see myself. Because I have chosen to dwell in a place you can't see.'

I see myself indulging in wanderlust; taking in the culture, people, history, and most importantly the food, from all over the world. Walking arm in arm, filled with wonder and passion and adventure with someone who shares this same thirst.

I see nights spent wrapped up in that other person, open, naked, and vulnerable; completely consumed by fire and desire—utterly exposed and unhindered sexuality. I see a partner who will make me laugh, smile, grow, lust, want, crave, be proud of what I have accomplished and who I am, all the time encouraging me to keep growing. I see deep conversations and an understanding of my ideas and perspectives whether he accepts it or not. I see someone who is willing to share my responsibilities, making me feel safe, secure, and most importantly, that I am not alone. I see freedom, where I have the security in knowing that I can make choices in the course and direction of my life in the areas of work, friendships, and interests without the fear of consequence or punishment from my partner. I see a man who views the world from a similar lens so just being and co-existing is effortless. I see a man who brings love, joy, affection, and empathy; someone who continually challenges me to grow and reach my full potential, and who is open and secure enough to grow with me. Not only that, he is empowered by my knowledge and understanding of the world. I want it to be instinctive the way he falls for me. Like an effortless intake of breath.

I see Sunday brunch surrounded by those who are able to see past the façade and accept all I am – all that makes me undeniably me. Brunches filled with laughter, children, friendships, genuine connection and ease of being. Brunches filled with delicious food, wine, and desserts. Always with an air of deep regard and authentic conversations.

With my children, I see strong bonds and secure attachments—an unspoken understanding of emotional safety and unconditional acceptance of one another. I see inside jokes and late night calls to announce life changing milestones. They will come to me with their heartbreaks and I will hold them while they share their deepest fears and concerns. I see playful banter and intellectual conversations; constantly challenging each other to learn and grow. I see family vacations and expansion of our little unit."

Although daydreaming or simply being able to eloquently articulate your vision will not be enough to catapult you into the life you are seeking, it is a start. We call this period an awakening because, more often than not, self-discovery is not about discerning or creating new goals or plans for your life, but about uncovering the essence of your desires and allowing yourself to embrace them. Being explicit about your expectations about love and the ways your lover will enhance your life and experiences keeps you grounded in the desires of your heart and makes it unlikely that you will settle for less.

Even though it may be painful to have to walk away from situations that seem adequate or acceptable, you are compelled to do so because you are awake to your dreams, passions and desires and settling for anything less will begin to feel wrong. You will begin to recognize the ways in which you may have sabotaged yourself in the past by settling for *good enough* and as a result, the work and patience required to move you to that next level of self-actualization will seem worthwhile and even compulsory.

***

Changing the Perceptions

"My life has been filled with terrible misfortunes, most of which have never happened."
—*Mark Twain*

It is inevitable that as we progress through this life, we will encounter times of misfortune and difficulty. In addition to external issues (e.g., work, social relationships), some of us may also struggle with physical or mental healthcare concerns that can make even seemingly small external difficulties feel monumental. At one time or another, you may have heard variations of statements or comments that are intended to be inspirational and helpful. Friends and loved ones, in honest attempts to make us feel better, oft utter such foolishness as 'cheer up', 'it's all in your head', 'let it go', or 'just think positive', as if we hadn't already tried everything in our power to will ourselves out of our funk or to move beyond our troubles.

I'm struggling even now to silence the frustration and annoyance resonating in my head. I know, in my spirit, that my friends and family aren't stupid, so how do they not assume that I've tried to think myself out of depression. They must know that I would give anything to just 'cheer up' and float to the top of my shithole instead of free-falling face first into personal hells, each one darker than the one before.

I want to lash out, to scream at them in the loudest voice that I can muster that 'this is not my fault'. I am not here in this place of despair because I am defective—although sometimes it feels like it. And although I am desperately in need of someone to throw me a life jacket, to help me to safety, they have to first understand that I am drowning. And if they are still telling me to just get my shit together, clearly they must think I am swimming in the deep end by choice and they are oblivious to the weights and chains that are making it difficult to move or breathe and that pull me further under the water. If I have learned anything in the last several decades, it is that I cannot rely on anyone else to see or understand 'what lies beneath' or even what lies within.

I have to figure out a way to move myself from the dark places and, although I wish it was true, thinking myself happy just isn't going to cut it.

Our brains are magnificent and have immense transformative power; however, they are also stubborn, resistant to change and determined to create patterns of behavior based on meanings. In order to fully utilize our 'brain power' to change our current moods and beliefs, we have to accept and attempt to harness both of these truths. This requires us to do more than just will it into existence. That being said, our brains do help us process our experiences in order to make sense of them and hopefully be able to call upon the lessons learned to help us achieve our goals. The brain has the ability to take new experiences, segregate them, and categorize them into schema—distinct frameworks created for the purpose of maintaining mental organization and clarity. Within each of these schemas, we create a frame of reference that helps us navigate subsequent similar experiences.

These frames constitute largely unquestioned beliefs and values which, once developed, are used when inferring meaning in subsequent situations (our worldview). Interestingly, if we experience even a small change in the frame, the meaning that we infer is likely to change, as well. This is the process referred to as reframing. We may not be able to fully let things go; we can't simply cheer up or get over them, but what we can do is to look at (and interpret) our situations using a different lens or new (revised) frame.

Take your morning commute for example; you leave your house 15 minutes earlier than usual and are quite proud of your exceptional organizational skills this given morning. You get on the road and after the first turn, you find yourself stuck on a one lane road behind a school bus. A school bus with a pick up schedule that requires it to stop what seems like every two houses—and you are fully aware of the laws so you know you cannot pass. So you wait…stopping every two houses, watching children say goodbye to parents and slowly board the bus. The inevitable result? You are late to the staff meeting that you

109

intended to arrive to early, in order to make a great impression on your new team lead. As you sit there, you experience an onslaught of familiar self-deprecating messages—negative feelings and conclusions you tell yourself about yourself. Our schemas and frames are often organized in such a way that something as simple as being stuck by a school bus and being a few minutes late to a meeting can elicit in us messages that make us question our planning skills, our inability to be on time or organized, and ultimately our worth. Sound familiar? In order for the thought process (or downward spiral of negative thoughts) to be different, our frames would need to be revised, because we are unlikely to arrive at a different outcome if we are using the old frame.

It will at times feel very difficult to stay positive or move on. Rest assured, by 'moving on' we don't mean ignoring a situation and taking on a Susie Sunshine demeanor; we mean avoiding denial or deflection and legitimately processing your feelings so that you can move to a new understanding. In these instances, try to step back and tune out (if possible) the chaos and negativity that is screaming inside and consider the frame in which this reality is being created. Remember that our frames are largely unquestioned and therefore unchallenged; we allow them to simply exist and alter our reality accordingly. In order to change or adjust our frames, we must consciously attempt to understand the unspoken assumptions and beliefs that underlie them.

> "To reframe then, means to change the conceptual and/or emotional setting or viewpoint in relation to which a situation is experienced and to place it in another frame which fits the 'facts' of the same concrete situation equally well or even better, and thereby changing its entire meaning."
> —Watzlawick, Weakland and Fisch (1974)

We assign meaning to situations by taking parts of the experience and intertwining them with messages we have received in the past. The most insidious messages are self-limiting beliefs that prevent you from accepting your full potential. These often manifest as some variation of the familiar fear that 'I'm not good enough', where the 'good' can be replaced by any other adjective that more adequately expresses our fears (e.g., pretty, smart, thin, worthy). Before you can start actively trying to reframe, it is critical that you recognize and acknowledge these negative beliefs.

A reframe is far more effective when you understand what's motivating the thought, because reframing leaves the facts alone and challenges the meaning you have assigned to them. In the previous example of being late on your morning commute, one may assign meanings such as 'I am such a screw up and I am incapable of getting my life together', or 'It doesn't matter how much I try, things will always go wrong', or 'my new team lead will think I'm a lazy, worthless part of this team'. Before you go all the way down the rabbit hole of self-loathing, look at the entire truth of the situation and then figure out which parts of the event you want to focus on. First, acknowledge the objective facts: despite your best efforts you were late and there may be consequences. The rest of the experience is meaningless, but it is equally as valid. The truth is that you did leave early which means you are taking steps to be more responsible and punctual. Another truth is that sometimes we will be caught in traffic and cannot (legally) do much to navigate around it, especially those of us in growing urban cities. The truth, again, is that your boss and coworkers have other examples of your work ethic and personality to draw from and this single event will not negate the image they hold.

By looking at the entire truth, you can work *with* your mind to create a positive reframe. In the beginning, this process of challenging the negative thoughts as they emerge will require conscious effort because it is unfamiliar. As you become more familiar with the process, you will find that it is far more effective than chastising yourself for having negative thoughts in the first place. Because, as we have worked meticulously to uncover, these thoughts are there and they rear their nasty little heads for a reason. Be aware of the messages and defense mechanisms while you are evaluating this situation.

I'm dressed and waiting. I check my makeup one last time and it is flawless. I silently commend myself. My hair is clean and in a top bun that would make a runway model jealous. I am ready. I watch the clock eagerly. It's 6:50. 10 more minutes and he'll be here. The date was his idea. I don't even know where we're going. I change shoes, deciding to wear my stilettos and hoping that we're able to find parking close by. 6:55. My phone buzzes. He must be close! I snap a selfie to post on social media with the hashtag #datenight. I am happy. I remember the incoming message and check to see how much time I have before he arrives.

He hasn't left his house. He says the weather is bad...can we postpone? I'm hurt but I refuse to show it. I acquiesce, "sure...another time!" I put down the phone and begin disrobing. Friday night takeout is nothing new to me...I shouldn't be upset, in fact it's often my favorite evening of the week because I get to relax alone and regroup. But this feels different. As I throw on sweats to go pick up something to eat, I feel abandoned. The voices are getting louder and I'm having a harder time ignoring them and thus fighting back the tears. I catch a glimpse of myself in the rearview mirror. He didn't show up because he found something better to do; you're not worth his time. You'll never find someone who puts you first and keeps their promises, because you're not worth it. Look at you, who would want you, you'll be alone forever... The loop runs through my head as I navigate the city... the sun shines. See, the weather is beautiful; he didn't want to go because YOU are not beautiful. I hear another voice...it's quieter than the messages and comes from somewhere different. IT feels like truth, it is calming and soft. It simply says 'challenge'. And I do. One by one, I confront the messages.

As we mentioned earlier, because we typically approach our schemas and frames with a 'business as usual' mindset deeply rooted in our subconscious, the act of challenging your thoughts may not feel intuitive. So, here are some basic questions you can ask yourself when you feel like the thoughts are taking over and you are able to recognize that you want them to stop and that you want to create a different reality.

- Am I trying to interpret this situation without looking at the entire event?
- What is the evidence that supports this thought?
- Is there any evidence contrary to this thought?
- How would my closest friend respond to this thought?
- Will this matter and will I remember the details about this issue in 6 months, a year or 5 years?

As you develop the skill of reframing, your questions will likely evolve, but this a good place to start. One of the benefits of undergoing a process like this is that it causes you to pause and question your assumptions instead of blindly believing them and letting them affect your reality.

***

Meditation

Similarly, coping techniques that involve visualization in some form help us focus on the inner mental experience, thereby fostering a relaxed state of mind. Guided imagery is one technique used with meditation that works to incorporate a person's senses in order to better direct and focus attention on a particular area of concern. Guided imagery can be defined as imagining a desired outcome for a given situation. Paul Dolan reminds us that "*your happiness is determined by how you allocate your attention. What you attend to drives your behavior and it determines your happiness. Attention is the glue that holds your life together...*"

Meditation, another helpful technique to focus your attention, can take many forms. While this mindfulness technique may conjure images of yogis chanting quietly in seemingly painful poses, the reality of meditation is much less rigid. Of course, there are the traditional forms where you use awareness and control of breathing and body movements (e.g., yoga), or meditation using imagery or repetitive calming or centering words or phrases (e.g., chanting). However, meditation can also take other nontraditional forms such as dancing, listening to music, muscle relaxation, or even cleaning. The overall goal is simply to quiet your mind and allow yourself to re-center and reconnect with yourself. Thus, it is up to you to explore and determine which method is most effective for you.

For those of you who may feel like the calm peaceful type of meditation doesn't resonate with you, storyteller Jason Headley provides us with a guided meditation session like no other. In a calm voice with the sounds of waves crashing in the background, Headley transports the listener to an effortless sense of awareness and calm, often intermixed with laughter and a good dose of mindfulness. "Sit or lie comfortably, quietly. Allow yourself to be here fully in this moment. With your eyes closed, begin to connect with your inner world of thought and feeling."

Unexpectedly and brilliantly, he showers expletives in the course of this meditation and with a burst of laughter, we are reminded that healing doesn't necessarily need to be rated PG. He urges us along the process...

> Take in a deep breath. Now breathe out.
> Just feel the fucking nonsense float away.
> Take full, deep breaths. Breathe in strength, breathe out bullshit.
> Allow your breathing to discover its own natural, unhurried pace. If your thoughts drift to the three-ring shit-show of your life, bring your attention back to your breathing. And with each breath, feel your body saying, 'Fuck that'.

We can and should call it like it is, even in our meditations and time of quiet reflection, and own what we are experiencing. If laughter is a source to process, relax and accept, well then all the better! There is true beauty in realizing that healing can be found in unexpected places.

Music is a wonderful example of finding healing in unexpected places. Many of us integrate music into our life, using it for recreation, relaxation or simply as a backdrop to block out the silence. However, we often fail to realize that music can also help us to process our emotions and inspire us to heal. If music as a source of healing resonates with you, then think of this as your *language of meditation.* The music will make you feel connected and like someone really 'gets' you. For those who have a harder time translating their feelings into words (a necessary step in processing), listening to certain songs can help you sift through your own feelings to better understand yourself and work through your emotions. The improved cognitive processing associated with listening to certain types of music (Neuroscience News) may lead an individual to move more efficiently from point A (feeling) to point B (resolution), instead of remaining stagnant.

As we move through life, we are guaranteed to have experiences that lead to intense feelings and emotions, whether it be conflict with a loved one, ending a relationship, or experiencing physical or emotional trauma. There are times when these experiences will humble us and bring us to our knees in pain, sadness, confusion, or some combination of undesirable emotions. Coping is the key to moving beyond that.

When attempting to use music as a form of coping, it will likely be necessary to draw from an eclectic array of genres in order to fully represent certain circumstances or emotions. Using music as a coping resource means listening beyond the catchy rhythms or melodic harmonies. It may even require us to venture away from our musical preferences. Thus, for someone who loves R&B or blues, healing from heartache may come in country western or blue grass. And for someone who prefers Top 40, coping with mental illness may be facilitated by an alternative artist with similar struggles. We must be open to this experience.

Unless you are already a diehard music fan with interests spanning different genres, it may be necessary to do some radio surfing or spend some time watching videos online. However you choose to go about it, it is helpful to develop a list of songs that speak to different circumstances and emotions that you experience. When developing your list, separating the songs into categories such as empowerment, frustration, sadness, and joy provide a quick point of reference when you're feeling a given emotion.

During tough life experiences, when you may lack the ability or desire to put your own feelings into words, music can be a constructive way to express who you are and what you are feeling. If you are feeling particularly sad, anxious, angry or confused about a reality in your life, listen to a song that connects you to that emotion. Often, we find that intellectual or verbal expressions of feelings are inadequate; if this is the case, connecting to the sadness, anxiety, or other emotion and giving it life in this manner helps you move through it. Allowing yourself to get lost in the music and be present in the emotion is one effective way to become more honest about what you are really experiencing.

My parents told me that I made this mistake with you once and that I better not make it with you again. They have forgiven me for this mistake of caring for you and to never do it again. I am sorry. I don't know how we will work out.

I draw in ragged breaths while reading his text message.

My world seems to be caving in. The room won't stop spinning. I can't breathe. My chest aches and I slowly sink to the floor.

Mistake.
I shake my head, desperate to be released from this treacherous hold. **You are a Mistake. You have been a mistake.**
For how long must I withstand this?

Mistake.
Please make it stop. I keep traveling in time. Flashes of memory play like a projector. **You were a mistake.** *I shake my head to rid myself of these before I lose myself completely in them. No, this is not it. No he didn't just say this... He couldn't have said this. I am not...I am...I am.*

And just as swiftly, I let myself go. Spasms of violent tears shatter through me. Stifled screams on which I keep choking. Rocking back and forth, alone. I am a mistake. I have always been a mistake.

Years of work and healing couldn't get rid of this one. Too many stitches, too many scars, now all gaping, bleeding and ripped anew.

I can't drown. The babies will be here soon. I can't let them see this. They don't deserve to see this. I need to make sense of all of this and get a hold of myself. I don't have much time...Music is my saving grace. The melodic ribbons swirl around me, cradling my head as I lose myself in the enchanting lyrics. These songs reflect my inner turmoil. She gets it. The pain. The rejection. The isolation.

"*Are you insane like me?*
Been in pain like me?
Bought a hundred dollar bottle of champagne like me?
Just to pour that motherfucker down the drain like me?
Would you use your water bill to dry the stain like me?
Are you high enough without the Mary Jane like me?
Do you tear yourself apart to entertain like me?
Do the people whisper 'bout you on the train like me?
Saying that you shouldn't waste your pretty face like me?
And all the people say
You can't wake up, this is not a dream
You're part of a machine, you are not a human being
With your face all made up, living on a screen
Low on self-esteem, so you run on gasoline
I think there's a flaw in my code
These voices won't leave me alone
Well my heart is gold and my hands are cold
Are you deranged like me?
Are you strange like me?
Lighting matches just to swallow up the flame like me?
Do you call yourself a fucking hurricane like me?"
                                                    —**Gasoline, Halsey**

*The howling, the desperation. I feel like I am watching myself from above. Why? Why now? My father told me once that my mother should have had an abortion...why? That sinister voice in my head is answering for me. **You were never wanted.** His life would have been easier, better, more fulfilled without me.*

"*Crawling in my skin*
These wounds, they will not heal
Fear is how I fall
Confusing what is real
There's something inside me that pulls beneath the surface
Consuming, confusing
This lack of self-control I fear is never ending
Controlling
I can't seem
To find myself again
My walls are closing in
(Without a sense of confidence I'm convinced
That there's just too much pressure to take)
I've felt this way before
So insecure
Discomfort, endlessly has pulled itself upon me
Distracting, reacting
Against my will I stand beside my own reflection
It's haunting how I can't seem
To find myself again
My walls are closing in
(Without a sense of confidence I'm convinced
That there's just too much pressure to take)
I've felt this way before
So insecure"

—Crawling, Linkin Park

The sobbing has slowed despite the ringing of my heartbeat in my ears. Panic has receded into a deep sorrow. Everything we have experienced up to this point, so easily cast aside and labeled a mistake. He is looking to leave. He wants out but is too cowardly to say it; instead he hides behind his mother's skirt. I shake my head at the fool I have allowed myself to become once again. Burnt by the same flame twice. I feel lightheaded. I feel myself swaying at the complete loss of vitality, of strength, of power. I take a deep breath.

"Why does it feel like night today?
Something in here's not right today
Why am I so uptight today?
Paranoia's all I got left
I don't know what stressed me first
Or how the pressure was fed
But I know just what it feels like
To have a voice in the back of my head
It's like a face that I hold inside
A face that awakes when I close my eyes
A face watches every time I lie
A face that laughs every time I fall
(And watches everything)
So I know that when it's time to sink or swim
That the face inside is hearing me
Right underneath my skin
It's like I'm paranoid lookin' over my back
It's like a whirlwind inside of my head
It's like I can't stop what I'm hearing within
It's like the face inside is right beneath my skin
I know I've got a face in me
Points out all my mistakes to me
You've got a face on the inside too and
Your paranoia's probably worse
I don't know what set me off first
But I know what I can't stand
Everybody acts like the fact of the matter is
I can't add up to what you can"
—Papercut, Linkin Park

I was there for you. I believed in you. I stood by you and held your hand. I was your lover, your confidant, your sounding board, your strength, your support, your teacher, your partner.

You were my new lease on life. You showed me I was lovable, worth chasing, you believed in me, you cared for me, you loved me…and just like that I am nothing. I am cast aside and discarded like yesterday's trash. I am the tarnish on your perfectly polished façade. So easily dismissed. Nothing to you. No value to you. Not worth fighting for.

"You were that foundation
Never gonna be another one, no.
I followed, so taken
So conditioned I could never let go
Then sorrow, then sickness
Then the shock when you flip it on me
So hollow, so vicious
So afraid I couldn't let myself see
That I could never be held
Back or up no, I'll hold myself
Check the rep, yep you know mine well
Forget the rest let them know my hell
There and back yet my soul ain't sell
Kept respect up, the best they fell,
Let the rest be the tale they tell
That I was there saying…
In these promises broken
Deep below
Each word gets lost in the echo
So one last lie I can see through
This time I finally let you
Go, go, go.
No, you can tell 'em all now
I don't back up, I don't back down
I don't fold up, and I don't bow
I don't roll over, don't know how
I don't care where the enemies are
Can't be stopped, all I know; go hard
Won't forget how I got this far
For every time saying…
In these promises broken

Deep below
Each word gets lost in the echo
So one last lie I can see through
This time I finally let you
Go."

—Lost in the Echo, Linkin Park

No. This is not acceptable. This is not okay. This is NOT who I have worked so hard to become. Too many years of trauma and I have floated around like a shell without a soul. I have cried and scratched and clawed my way through it and I am who I am now in SPITE of that. I will not be discarded. I am not to be dismissed. I am valued, I am loved, I am proud, I am worthy. I am NOT anyone's mistake!

"I need more dreams
And less life
And I need that dark
In a little more light
I cried tears you'll never see
So fuck you, you can go cry me an ocean
And leave me be
You are what you love
Not who loves you
In a world full of the word yes
I'm here to scream
NO!"

—Save Rock & Roll, Fall Out Boy

Your coping skills, how you move through trauma, will change over time. The same thing that comforted you through childhood may no longer work. The music that got you through the dissolution of a relationship may be inadequate when working through the loss of a loved one. The goal here isn't to find 'the perfect' solution because inevitably as situations change (even in incremental ways), what works will also change. And, as you grow, your coping skills with have to grow and evolve with you.

121

No matter how you chose to cope, the important part is that you are actively attempting to move through the experience. Again, we want to point out our use of the term 'move through' instead of 'move on', because that is what processing is! You can't just 'get over things' without going through and understanding them. And, inevitably, there may be experiences in your life that are so monumental, so earth-shakingly bad, so traumatic, that you never truly move on and leave them in the past. These experiences you will simply learn to coexist with, without letting them destroy you or wreak havoc on your present.

Regardless of the method you chose to employ to move through your experience, set a time limit when processing your thoughts and feelings so as not to get overwhelmed. Start with 5 or 10 minutes and increase the time if necessary. Tune in to what is going on in your body. Feeling a bit of anxiety and apprehension is normal—especially when this is still new to you—but if you feel that you are pushing too hard and you find yourself resistant to the process, it's okay to back off for a time, until you feel more ready. When your allotted time is up, return from the exclusive processing of what is going on in your body, revisit your thoughts and feelings. If you need more time, allot more time later in the day or on another day, but make sure you return to the process so that you can arrive at a resolution.

The reason why we suggest setting a time limit is because as important as it is to process experiences, staying in the 'going through it' phase too long can quickly turn to wallowing in pain and negativity and actually end up being unhealthy, both mentally and emotionally. The goal is to process and resolve and make sense of your experiences in order to heal from them, not to continue allowing them to negatively affect you. Although we rarely subject ourselves to pain willingly, you can grow from such experiences in your past and use them to your advantage. In times of strife or newly-discovered, and sometimes painful truths, use what you have learned to pause, center, and re-discover your true voice.

***

Relaxation Techniques

How often have you said or thought: I need to relax. There may be nothing in particular going on (or wrong), no major life event that is bothering you, but in general, we live busy, stressful lives. Whether our motivation is to relieve stress or simply be more present in the moment, sometimes we just need to relax. It is as close to a universal truth as we can get that no one can avoid all stress. Although the psychological sciences teach us that there are two types of stress, eustress and distress, we are focusing here on distress—the more negative manifestation. Because stress is virtually inevitable, we find it necessary to learn strategies to invoke our body's natural *relaxation response,* a state of deep rest that is the polar opposite of the stress response. Once enacted, we can use the relaxation response to combat the negative emotional and physical effects of stress.

The idea of returning to a present orientation during times of stress can be referred to a grounding, or connecting to a solid foundation which can change, and often decrease, the intensity of our emotional reactions. For times when you are or feel yourself becoming overwhelmed—whether with your job, children, relationship, or distressing memories, thoughts and feelings—the relaxation response returns your body and mind to a state of equilibrium by giving yourself an opportunity to realign. The following grounding exercises are about using our five senses (i.e., sight, smell, hearing, taste, and touch) to enhance our mind and body connection in the present.

Progressive muscle relaxation, a popular method used to ground oneself, uses breathing and imagery to realign the mind and body and decrease our negative or distressful emotional reactions. When you are ready to try this technique, find a comfortable place where you can be undisturbed for several minutes. If you are physically able, sit cross-legged on the floor or ground. If not, find a comfortable chair that allows you to sit straight up and place your bare feet on the ground or earth. The imagery is enhanced when you have this physical connection to the solid ground or earth and becomes more effective in moving us towards feeling grounded.

Now that you're comfortable, breathe in deeply, and hold this breath. Hold it until you feel like you have to breathe again, this is often a second after it becomes uncomfortable...now release. With your eyes still closed, try to envision your silhouette sitting just as you are at this moment. It might be difficult at first, but try to feel your presence and find the outline of your body. Without assigning meaning, pay attention to the colors within and around your silhouette. Much like other strategies, there is no right or wrong way to do this and it might differ from one time to the next. The important aspect here is to find yourself within your mind's eye. Each time I have done this exercise, I have conjured a different image. Most times, when I finally am able to envision myself, it is a dark color of brown, grey, or completely black.

Once you are able to find your outline, try to imagine that you are sitting on the ground and there are tree roots wrapped around your legs connecting you to the ground. Take a moment to enjoy this sensation. Roots are a source of nourishment and cleansing; they represent a secure attachment to the earth and prevent a tree from swaying or collapsing in the midst of a storm. Grounding yourself is meant to operate in much the same way.

Now, slowly take another deep breath and release the air slowly. If this feels difficult, try breathing in for six counts and breathing out for eight. As you release the air, let all the tension that you feel in your body go, as well. It may take one or more deep breaths like this to feel the tension start to exit. You will know that you have released the tension when the muscles in your body begin to loosen. Notice how relaxed the muscles feel now. Reflect on the difference between tension and relaxation. Enjoy the pleasant feeling of relaxation in yourself.

Focus back on your silhouette. Has it become clearer? Have the colors around you or within you changed? Can you find a light source somewhere? It often comes either from the top or sides of your image. Take your time. We are going to use this light source to start to shift and move your energy allowing it to flow through your body and into the ground through your new roots.

Take another deep breath. Hold it until you have to release and then slowly exhale. And, again. This time, pushing on the top of your head as you breathe in fully, let the breath expand your core. Hold it…and release the breath as well as the pressure. Next let's move down to your forehead. With another deep breath I want you to scrunch your forehead and make it tense. Hold the breath. Focus on the image of yourself, and as you release the tension with your breath, imagine pushing the energy within you from the top of your head down past your forehead. Imagine the light source within you spreading as you exhale. As you move on, breathe in and tighten the muscles of your face. Scrunch your eyes shut tightly, wrinkle your nose, and tighten your cheeks and chin. Hold the breath and this tension in your face...now relax. Release all the tension. Next focus on your neck and shoulders. Raise them forcefully to your ears and tighten the muscles. As you release your breath, let go of the muscles and feel the light float further down as you push the toxins through the roots in the ground. Breathe. Now focus on the muscles in your arms. Tighten your upper arms, lower arms, and hands. Squeeze your hands into tight fists. Tense the muscles in your arms and hands as tightly as you can. Hold the tension in your arms, shoulders, and hands. Feel the tension in these muscles. Hold it for a second longer...and now release. Let the muscles of your shoulders, arms, and hands relax and go limp. Feel the relaxation as your shoulders lower into a comfortable position and your hands relax at your sides. Breathe. Tighten the muscles of your back. Pull your shoulders back and tense the muscles along your spine. Arch your back slightly as you tighten those muscles. Hold, exhale and relax. Let all the tension go. Feel your back comfortably returning to a neutral and healthy posture. Turn your attention now to the muscles of your chest and stomach. Breathe. Tighten and tense these muscles. When you need to exhale, do so, slowly relaxing your core muscles. Move on to the muscles in your legs. Breathe, tighten them one at a time or all at once. Hold this tension and the breath...and release. Finally, with a purposeful and cleansing intake of breath, take a moment to re-focus on your image. Hold it, the breath. And with your final exhale whisper aloud, 'I am free'.

Examine what you saw in your mind's eye. What were the colors within and around you at the end of the grounding exercise? Had they changed from the beginning? Was the light brighter? The colors more vibrant? How do you feel?

Everything hurts. It's been a week from hell and every part of my body is a screeching reminder. I feel the heaviness in my soul and I know it is reflected in my eyes. People say I look tired. There are two forms of tired. The one where the physical body needs a rest; then there is the one where your spirit needs a rest. I feel both are needed at this point. So I sit down on my bedroom floor and begin the cleansing. I close my eyes and see nothing. I am trying to imagine myself sitting...It is all black. I cannot find myself at all. The surrounding areas of what would be my silhouette resemble a thick, impenetrable fog. I sit and breathe. It's not surprising to me that I cannot find myself given how lost and hopeless I have been feeling. I sit and as I take deep breaths I search with deliberate intent. I will not be lost. I am here, I am okay; I will make it. I am not lost. Finally after what seems like forever, I see an iridescent black figure within all of the overpowering darkness. Okay, at least I can start with that. Another slow deep breath, partly because that is what I am supposed to do, and partly because in all the times I have done this, it didn't take this long. I pull myself out from deep within my consciousness and force myself to focus on my silhouette. Now, where's that damn light source? It is so complicated at this point and I really just want to give it up and come back to it later. The only reason I do not is because I know this struggle is a true reflection of my inner turmoil. I will become lost if I don't work through this. The challenges I am facing in my existence is making me question everything I have worked tirelessly to overcome. On the very edges of my sight I find a lighter corner. There! Okay, (sigh) here we go! I inhale and start the progressive relaxation. As I go through the process from the top of my head, I feel the physical response. I feel the areas I hadn't noticed before. Like the space on either side of my spine, in between the shoulder blades. I feel it there. It takes until I get to my pelvis before the image gets noticeably lighter. I am no longer all black even though the fog is still stifling. With the final breath I notice the change in my silhouette. It is iridescent and sifting vibrantly while changing hues. I have never seen it this way. Even though the negativity in the external world feels stronger, I am not lost. I am present and vibrant and powerful. I have within me all that I need to be triumphant.

***

Journaling

Many of the strategies we have presented throughout the book have been simple suggestions that we know to be helpful (often from personal experiences). We have purposefully presented these strategies and suggestions in the form of a buffet, because we feel that it is essential that you are able to pick and choose what works best for you. Grounding can be one such strategy in your back pocket to help you along this journey; It doesn't have to manifest in exactly the same manner we outlined above; you will develop a method that works well for you. What is important is that throughout your journey, you remain connected to your inner truth. Without that you will quickly forget who you are, where you are going, and how far you have already come. Grounding gives you perspective and requires a recognition of your personal strengths.

Unfortunately, much like everything else in this journey, the process of grounding is one that we will have to do many times. The grounding process will be repeated not because we are ineffective but because the world and all of our circumstances will continue to change and to shake your foundation. It is easy to become discouraged. Journaling, another strategy to help keep you grounded, can help you to keep a running dialogue with yourself to make sense of things and also remind you of your journey and destination. Therefore, it can work hand-in-hand with your attempts to remain grounded.

Research has shown that requiring individuals to consciously recognize and attempt to verbally categorize emotions could reduce the impact of the emotions (Korb, 2012 *The Grateful Brain*). Writing about anger, sadness and other painful emotions helps us to process and thereby release the intensity of these feelings. Moreover, writing about stressful events helps you come to terms with them, thus reducing the impact of these stressors on your physical health (Pennebaker, 2004 *Writing to Heal)*. The science behind this is simple: the physical act of writing accesses your left brain, which is analytical and rational. While your left brain is occupied, your right brain is free to create, intuit and feel in order to more fully understand yourself, others and the world around you. Aside from the neurological benefits, there are other more practical benefits to keeping a narrative of your experiences. It will help clarify your thoughts and feelings.

By writing routinely you will get to know what makes you feel happy and confident. You will also become clear about situations and people who repeatedly bring conflict into your life. When a particular circumstance appears to be insurmountable, you will be able to look back on previous dilemmas that you have since resolved and draw inspiration for how to proceed. This is a great way to also pay attention to patterns of behaviors, which will help you focus in on how you resolve issues and bring awareness to personal or relational interactions.

If you are new to journaling, start with just writing down three positive things that happened today. Feel free to start out using a bulleted list as we have done previously; as you become more comfortable, work towards expanding your description of each of these positive experiences or events. As that becomes effortless, you can add a lesson learned or something you may have struggled with or learned to appreciate. Your appreciation can be about personal growth or about something about a specific person in your life.

Even if your last experience with journaling was your childhood diary, this experience will be different, and more useful. The process will be very personal and will require an increasing self-awareness over time as you delve deeper into your feelings, but it should also be a helpful resource for you. Aside from helping you to achieve or maintain clarity, journaling regularly gives you a record of your growth. I frequently find journals that I kept in college, graduate school, or during particularly difficult or intense life transitions, and after reading a few entries, I am able to see growth and progress, further reminding me that no matter what I may feel in an instant, I am strong and capable and the best of me is yet to come.

Masterpiece, Jessie J.

I still fall on my face sometimes
And I can't color inside the lines
Cause I'm perfectly incomplete...
No, you haven't seen the best of me
I'm still working on my masterpiece

6. Conclusion
So, Now What?

I hope that in working through this book, you were able to find your personal truths. These truths will be different for all of us, and may even be different for you from one reading of the book to the next. Among other self-discoveries, we hope that you discovered the truth behind what makes you feel most alive. Although this may not, at first glance, seem like the most important truth that lies within, it is essential for progress and growth towards your ideal self. And, sadly, it is one of the first things the world strips from us through a constant barrage of negative images and interactions. Once you have discovered that *fire*, our goal was that you have been able to harness the power that is inherent within you to identify the life or circumstances that you desire and that you have found a path to bringing this to fruition instead of pretending like those desires don't exist or that you don't deserve what you want.

We hope, by now, that you have discovered that we have made every attempt to be intentional with language throughout this book and our use of words like 'pretending' and 'creating' are no different. We hope that you have begun to use a lexicon, both with yourself and with others, that has the ability to demonstrate that you have the power, the right, and the resources, to create and weave your own narrative. This story, your story, is solely yours to create. For we are all but a tapestry woven by similar threads. Don Miguel Ruiz reminds us that others are simply extras in the movies of our lives and that we are the main characters. We hope that you feel encouraged to take the lead.

It is entirely up to you to determine which version of yourself you are willing to embrace and share with the world. We recognize the courage that is required to transform yourself into or realign yourself with that image. It may seem a scary and daunting task, but recognize that at this point you have already allowed yourself to push past your fears and embrace the person looking back at you in the mirror. You have faced the brutal truths that have been lurking in the shadows for what, for some, may seem an eternity, and reworked them into your personal totem and source of strength. When the familiar doubt or feelings that you are incapable of moving to that next step or milestone grips you, remember that you are powerful, lovable, beautiful, courageous, and magical. You are all you need to be and have it within you to become who you want to be.

You can write your true narrative IF you can dare to look past the surface. Although you will undoubtedly have responsibilities and obligations that extend beyond finding your best self, always keep yourself a priority. We implore you to remember the famous Shakespeare quote: "this above all; to thine own self be true." Because, at the end of the day, it is almost a certainty, that you will regret not living authentically.

We have delved through the painful elements of our human experience, the reasons why we relied on them, how and why we functioned as we have, and navigated through the difficult aspects of the human condition. With this new understanding, comes true growth. Whatever your truth is, live it, own it, and share it. It is your unique truth that makes you beautifully bare and undeniably you.

"Having perfected our disguise, we spend our lives searching for someone we don't fool."

—**Robert Brault**